Journeys into Palliative Care
Roots and Reflections

Edited by Christina Mason

Jessica Kingsley Publishers
London and Philadelphia

The extract from *The Cocktail Party* by T.S Eliot, p.161, appears by kind permission of
Faber and Faber Ltd. *Truly Great* by Stephen Spender, p.49–50, appears by kind
permission of Faber and Faber Ltd and the estate of the author.

First published in the United Kingdom in 2002
by Jessica Kingsley Publishers Ltd
116 Pentonville Road
London N1 9JB, England
and
325 Chestnut Street
Philadelphia, PA 19106, USA

www.jkp.com

Copyright © Jessica Kingsley Publishers 2002

Library of Congress Cataloging in Publication Data
Journeys into palliative care : roots and reflections / edited by Christina Mason.
    p. ; cm.
  Includes bibliographical references and index.
  ISBN 1-84310-030-4 (alk. Paper)
    1. Terminal care--Anecdotes. 2. Palliative treatment. 3. Terminally ill. 4. Reflections.
  I. Mason, Christina, 1942-
[DNLM: 1. Health Personnel--Personal Narratives. 2. Palliative Care--Personal Narratives.
WB 310 J86 2002]
R726.8 .J685 2002
362.1'75--dc21

                                                                    2002016237
British Library Cataloguing in Publication Data
A CIP catalogue record for this book is available from the British Library

ISBN 1 84310 030 4

Printed and Bound in Great Britain
by Athenaeum Press, Gateshead, Tyne and Wear

Contents

This book is dedicated to
St. Joseph's Hospice and all those
associated with it since
its beginning in 1905.

Acknowledgements

I want to thank a number of people who have directly and indirectly been involved in the writing of this book.

First and most obviously are those who have willingly contributed a chapter and worked with me over the past year to bring the book to completion.

Second, and perhaps less obviously, are those clients and patients whose stories have been told in various places throughout the book and from whom we have learned so much during the course of our careers.

I also acknowledge the people, too many to name individually, who have influenced my professional development. Their knowledge, skill and wisdom have been my source of inspiration.

I thank Marian Le Petit, who has been an invaluable help in preparing the manuscript, and I also thank my colleagues at St Joseph's Hospice for their continuing support and friendship. Jessica Kingsley Publishers have been helpful in advising on a number of editorial issues and I thank them most sincerely for their enthusiasm and acceptance of my ideas.

Finally, I want to acknowledge the love and encouragement of my partner, Robin, and my dear daughter, Jo.

Introduction

Christina Mason

In 1905 five religious Sisters of Charity made the journey from Ireland to care for the sick and give succour to the poor of the East End of London. This small group of women founded St Joseph's Hospice and here they looked after people who were suffering from the then prevalent infectious diseases, particularly tuberculosis, scourge of early twentieth-century families. Today, although alerted to the rising number of infections that have become resistant to antibiotics, the conditions which patients are suffering from when they arrive at St Joseph's are mainly the cancers, but also multiple sclerosis, motor neurone disease and some other long-term illnesses.

Many of the people coming into St Joseph's Hospice for the first time remark on how surprisingly light it is, and then on the polished floors and how wonderfully spotless they are. From the start, people feel welcomed. Visitors walk down the corridor and see photographs on the wall of the many and varied activities of the hospice. Someone has just done a parachute jump, and the person seen on the corridor yesterday is suddenly portrayed seemingly suspended two miles up and flying. There are pictures of the latest staff leaving party to which a beautiful baby has come, being admired by everyone. There are photographs of our oldest patient's 101st birthday and friends have come from far and wide to help in the party. In the midst of caring for people who are dying, we are also celebrating life in all its richness and variety.

This book too is a celebration, at least in part. It is a way of recognising that at St Joseph's we are coming near to our centenary. As the year 2005 approaches, we are reflecting on all the patients, staff and relatives whose lives have been touched by the hospice and who have contributed knowledge, skills and understanding in the care of people who are dying. We remember and celebrate the many human gifts that over the years we have enjoyed in the service and care of people who are very ill, dying, or in sorrow following the death of someone deeply loved.

During these hundred years of history there have been many changes in the way that medicine and health care in general are practised. One of the changes, which is relevant to this book, is the development and growth of a specialty around the care of persons who are very seriously ill and reaching the end of their lives. The foundations of this specialty were laid at St Joseph's Hospice and the other hospices that were caring for people who were dying at the turn of the twentieth century. As the century advanced there were further advances in pain and symptom control with major contributions being made by Dame Cicely Saunders and other pioneers in the field. Such specialist care is now known as palliative care and it became an accredited medical specialty in 1987.

A general definition of palliative care might be that it is the total care of patients and also their families by a multi-professional team when the condition of the patient no longer responds to treatments aimed at cure. The goal of palliative care is the achievement of a good quality of life and it offers support to patients in living actively for as long as possible until death. Respect for patients is paramount. This includes their being able to choose where to die, and to be full participants in decisions about treatment options. These treatments aim to relieve distressing pain, nausea, breathlessness, depression, anxiety and other varied symptoms that frequently accompany the last phase of serious illness.

A central component of palliative care is that the family is fully involved, and support of family members both before and after their relatives die is taken very seriously indeed. Attention is also given to friends and neighbours: people who have been important in patients' lives. Palliative care is integrated care. The physical, emotional, social and spiritual aspects of a person's life are considered of equal importance and it is a core assumption that unrelieved distress in one of these aspects will affect all others. Hence the importance of multi-professional teams of doctors, nurses, social workers, physiotherapists, chaplains and spiritual advisors, dieticians and complementary therapists. Such a team works together *and* with the patient and family to provide treatments, support, information, advice and sometimes very practical help as appropriate to the needs and wishes of the patient.

I spent a long time over the title of this book. There was so much that I wanted to express about the work of palliative care and the connections between those who provide and those who receive it. Roots, in the title, conjure up many images: trees and plants burrowing deep into the earth and giving nourishment, stability and security to the growing plant; the root of a word or a tooth, something fundamental and indispensable. Our roots as human beings are, I believe, equally influential, even though sometimes we might feel 'rootless' and insecure. The overwhelming majority of us as human beings have become what we are today because of our roots, what we learned throughout childhood, directly through teaching, indirectly through example and modelling. Then there are the other sorts of routes that we travel on our way to a chosen career and which are strongly influenced, even though not always recognised, by environmental experiences and chance events as well as parental ambitions and example. That is the core of this book; accounts of how experienced professionals found their way into palliative care and related areas and the influence of their particular paths on the way they work. These echo the journeys of people as they are approaching the ends of their lives.

Several sources of inspiration lay behind the book. First, I suppose, is the recurring reaction of people to information about where I work. I have been at St Joseph's Hospice for the past six years, but the seeds of the book began to germinate when I told people in the little Perthshire village where I used to live that I was moving to East London to work with people who were dying. My announcement was greeted with shocked expressions and rather wry remarks about my eccentricity. Since then people have frequently asked, 'What led you to work in this area? Isn't it terribly depressing seeing people dying? How do you cope with it all?'

Good questions indeed. What *does* lead people into palliative care as their chosen area of work and how do we manage the feelings involved when, day by day, the people we have cared for, die? I hope that the accounts given in these chapters might provide some answers to these questions.

The second inspiration behind this book was an academic sociologist who was my mentor some years ago. He was a wonderful person – unassuming, loved by his students and generous with his time and support. When he died from a heart attack there were many people who mourned his passing. He had co-edited a book, to which he had contributed a chapter, on personal accounts of illness analysed from a sociological perspective. He taught me how personal experience can be reflected upon from a theoretical perspective and in a way that can enlarge everyone's understanding.

That enabled me to understand more readily what has become known amongst professionals in a number of different disciplines as 'reflective practice' when much later I was training in social work. There *is* reflection in this book – personal reflection on life and death and the way in which biography influences professional practice in so many different and sometimes surprising ways.

The third influence on this book was the work that I did for my doctoral thesis in the late 1970s and early 1980s. The research was stimulated by a problem of communication in a hospital setting. Apart from the fieldwork part of the research, I was steeped in literature about communication and some of the problems experienced by both recipients and providers of care. I have retained a passionate interest in this area of study, the source of problems and suggested remedies. Part of the thesis of *this* book is connected with ways to tackle communication difficulties. There has been an increasing recognition that the personal attributes of a professional are as important to the work of healing as the skills learned during education and training. These attributes include the life experiences, the preferences, the motivations, as well as the gifts, knowledge and skills of professional carers; things which make each of us different from the other; things which we bring with us into the consulting room, clinic or home when we are visiting those who are sick. There are many texts on this subject, and it is called various things – counter-transference in the psychotherapy literature, for example. I shall refer from time to time to transference issues, but I go beyond this to consider what I call the 'use of the self' in the process of caring for, or doing research with, people who are troubled and in pain.

I have invited a number of practitioners in different disciplines, from various parts of Britain and one from Australia, to reflect on three questions: What are the roots of your interest in palliative care? What route did you take into the discipline? What has been the effect of your particular journey on the work you do with the dying and grieving? The disciplines represented are medicine, nursing, social work, psychology, psychotherapy, creative writing, research and education. The results of these reflections are nine chapters written by people who have substantial experience of working with those who are dying, those who are in despair and those who are struggling with various kinds of losses. The authors reflect on key issues and often ask questions about their practice such as, the management of one's own distress when working in an area so full of poignancy, the ethical issues faced in palliative care and how these are dealt with, sharing sorrow at loss, the management of denial in patients and their families and several other topics.

The book will highlight a number of theoretical themes and these include the following. I discuss 'the use of self', a concept from both social work and psychotherapy, particularly with reference to the person-centred tradition. Counter-transference will be described and some of the literature explored, especially in working with people who are seriously ill and when there may be an absence of understanding of one's own history. The importance of story-telling, both for the client and the professional, and the use of story and metaphor as a therapeutic tool will also be introduced.

Today palliative care principles are finding their way into general professional practice. Far from being the minority discipline it may once have been, people are recognising just how much can be learned and applied from the philosophy and practice of palliative care. The book has a purpose, and that is to encourage readers, whether they are practitioners in palliative care or working in other areas, to reflect on the way they use the self in their work, and if they do not, are there any ways, having read the accounts of experienced practitioners, that their personal attributes and histories can be used to good effect in their practice. I want the book to be helpful for practitioners who are struggling with practice issues, and to be of interest to anyone who enjoys good stories!

In the first chapter, I shall be examining some of the theoretical literature on the use of self, and I shall be looking at some aspects of professional socialisation prior to the personal accounts, which are contained in chapters two to ten. In chapter two, Louis Heyse-Moore, who is the medical director of St Joseph's Hospice, examines some of his various experiences as a child, young person and in early adulthood and the way these have impacted on his career and his chosen field of practice as a doctor. Chapter three finds Julia Franklin, now retired from full-time social work practice, describing the early days of palliative care as a major specialty and the many new things that were challenging and which required different approaches to practice. Personal discovery and its impact on therapeutic practice is the overarching theme of chapter four, written by Robin Trewartha, a chartered counselling psychologist who has worked for many years with people experiencing major losses and traumas. Chapter five describes how its author, Gillie Bolton, found her way into creative writing and the use she makes of this form of expression in her work with both patients and staff in palliative care. This chapter is followed by one in which David Oliviere, an experienced social work practitioner and now an educator of palliative care professionals in all disciplines, traces his first formative experiences of loss and shows through case studies the way in which these remain influential many years later. Lois Pollock began her career in Australia and in chapter seven she gives an account of her work in several different countries and the way in which her spirituality has been a guiding influence on her practice with people who are dying. Gordon Riches is a researcher, academic and writer on the theme of loss of children and the pain of this experience for parents, siblings and other family members. In chapter eight he describes the impact of his research work on himself, and the way in which he has come to see aspects of his own biography as being influential. I have contributed chapter nine myself and I write from the perspective of both social worker and psychotherapist on the slow steady unfolding of a vocation to work with the dying and grieving. The final autobiographical chapter has been written by a nurse who is now director of nursing at St Joseph's Hospice. He describes the way in which a very significant and terribly painful personal loss led him to recognise the importance for all professionals of reflecting deeply on their practice and the various influences on it. Chapter eleven ends the book and is a review of the main points that I think emerge from these accounts and also some exercises, which may be useful for further reflection.

1

Basic themes

Christina Mason

Introduction

In this chapter I introduce the underlying thesis of the book, drawing on work from the early 1960s to the present day. Quite a lot of this literature comes from research on medical practice but the overall thesis is intended to relate to all professional carers and not just medical practitioners. Because the book is intended for a multi-professional readership, I use the words 'client' and 'patient' interchangeably, the intention being to refer to recipients of care whether that care is given by doctors, nurses, social workers or other therapists.

Communication problems identified

From the early 1960s and emanating from a number of different disciplines, articles in professional journals and books on the subject of communication breakdown in health care began to be published and this literature has continued to the present day (Freidson 1961; Bloom 1963; Fletcher 1973; Pendleton and Hasler 1983; Weatherall 1994; Kirklin and Richardson 2001).

An example of one such work is that of Byrne and Long (1976), who analysed 2500 audio recordings of 71 doctors speaking with patients. They identified seven communication styles based on a shift in power from that centred on the doctor to that which was focused more on the patient. Thus the doctor-centred style would include direct, closed, self-answering questions and justifying chastising behaviour. By contrast the patient-centred style would seek out and use a patient's ideas, reflect, clarify, indicate understanding, and use silence. The majority of doctors were found to practise at the doctor-centred end of the spectrum. My own research found similar patterns of communication. This was conducted in an out-patient clinic for people with diabetes. The tape recordings of 91 patients talking with a physician, dietician and social worker showed that only in the case of the social worker was there space for patients to ask questions and to respond to what they were feeling about being ill with this condition (Mason 1984).

The *effect* of different styles of communication on users of services has also been reported in several places. For example, the personal anguish arising from a policy of 'not telling' is well reflected in the following verse from a poem written by a woman as she approached the end of her days.

> The surgeon comes with student retinue,
> mutters to sister, deaf to my silent plea,
> I want to tell this dread I feel inside
> but they are all too kind to talk to me.
> (Anonymous. Quoted in Twycross, 1975)

More recently, Michele Petrone, describing his very mixed experience of cancer therapy, has said that it is 'not just treatment which cures you, but all that encompasses the human touch' (Petrone 2001). A series of articles was published in the *British Medical Journal* written by patients who had had a variety of difficult experiences, all of which stemmed from doctors' absence of sensitivity (Weatherall 1994).

Byrne and Long (1976) had asked the question 'How do styles come to be formed?', and in the next few paragraphs I shall attempt to identify some of the formative factors that have been suggested. One view is that styles begin to develop early as a result of role modelling; for instance, observing health professionals when ill, having a relative who works as a nurse or doctor, and later watching teachers while in training. Another view is that, as far as doctors are concerned, they have been receiving teaching that draws attention to the physiological at the expense of the social, the diagnosis of disease at the expense of its management, with hours of time spent learning about deviations from normal physiology (Metcalfe 1983). And as the twentieth century continued, the pressure on health care practitioners appeared to become even greater with high technology medicine, ever more information to assimilate, but very little time for reflection.

In this context of priorities, the emotional aspects of illness tend to be overlooked (Duff and Hollingshead 1968).

> By applying his medical vocabulary of disease with its main emphasis on bodily functioning, the physician may well lose sight of the fact that illness affects social ways of acting, and that for the ill person, the degree to which his social functioning and way of life are affected is his main immediate concern. (Field 1976, p.355)

It has been argued that students do not develop the skills to see beyond the physiology to what is more difficult to define, the feelings and reactions of individual sufferers that are always present, crucially affecting the course of the illness.

But such educational experiences are not the only formative factors in communication styles. There are others.

First, communication in health care systems occurs in the context of a bureaucracy that has its own structure and goals. One of these goals is that people be processed speedily and efficiently. A professional-centred style could be seen as highly functional in such contexts.

Second, Strong (1977), in a hospital observational study, noted the way in which practitioners refer to patients as 'customers' and the work as 'trade', or 'business', as in any other mass service organisation. The queue of patients is part of the ordinary routine of work. The style of communication adopted is influenced by the ordinariness of the work (Tate 1983).

There is also the authority invested in physicians by patients. Holohan (1977) describes a vivid example of the strength of this investment. She was in hospital for biopsy examination of a breast lump. During her stay she observed the sanctions imposed by other patients on a woman who resisted medication. She writes:

> The authority vested in the profession was sacrosanct. Her 'deviation' ended, as one patient said, 'when she came to her senses and agreed'. Clearly we had impinged on deeply held social norms. The patient comes to the doctor, places himself in his hands, follows his orders and this trust will be rewarded by skilled therapeutic intervention.

This was felt to be appropriate, proper and morally right, and 'the community' as represented by other patients strongly supported these expectations and obligations. So strongly did they feel, that these acts were not mere infractions of social rules, but symptoms of illness. (Holohan 1977, p.94)

The final factor relating to communication styles that I identify is rather different although it is certainly influenced by the context of practice. It is this factor that will be the subject of more attention in the remainder of the chapter. The eighteenth-century surgeon anatomist William Hunter (c.1780) urged his students to gain 'a necessary inhumanity' by dissecting the dead. Perhaps this kind of rite of passage into a profession might have been necessary when anaesthesia was not available, for the control of patient input in the psycho-social sphere may have been thought necessary for practitioners' own protection at this time. However, for decades following, there seems to have been a tendency in the education of health professionals to train out the personal and emotional responses of practitioners to the suffering they were witnessing. A rather striking and recent example of this is that of a general practitioner who declined to be involved in a research study into the emotional demands of general practice. He stated that it was a waste of time because emotions are not a part of a general practitioner's professional life (Frost and King 2000).

Despite this statement, I would suggest that as part of the practice of health care, situations will be encountered which are personally emotionally challenging and distressing for staff and until very recently, little opportunity has been offered during their years of training for students to explore their own feelings about disease, suffering and death. Some, on graduation, become overwhelmed (Merrison 1975; Murray 1983). Others adopt various defence mechanisms, including turning off to matters that cannot be handled. As Metcalfe (1983) suggests, denial (that they feel inadequate) is used as a coping strategy by many health professionals. In these circumstances, they need to control situations in order to manage the uncertainty and perplexity that are inherent in the clinical role.

Attempts to find remedies

Recognising some of these difficulties, at least as they relate to doctors, the General Medical Council in 1993 suggested a major change of curriculum, with 30 per cent of the timetable to be allocated to special study modules in, amongst other things, medical humanities (GMC 1993). The humanities place the expression, exploration and interpretation of the human condition as central to human philosophical and artistic endeavour (Hurwitz 2000).

Underlying this report and its recommendations is the idea, dating back to Hippocrates (Chadwick and Mann 1950), that the practice of medicine is an art. There appear to be three purposes to the study of humanities: to enable students to understand the experience and perspectives of patients; to examine motivations underlying professional practice; and to connect through a shared humanity with individuals coming for care (Kirklin and Richardson 2001).

It appears that what is being suggested here is a form of reflective practice, an opportunity for professionals to examine thoughts, feelings, inclinations and life experience that impact on therapeutic practice and a chance to gain new insights into the strengths and weaknesses of their work (Schon 1983, 1987). This idea of reflective practice is not new for social workers or counsellors; in medicine and nursing its history is shorter.

The recommendations of the GMC also bring to the forefront the long-term recognition that one of the most important aspects of healing is the relationship which exists between the healer and the one who is requiring to be healed. For example, Egbert (1964) found that pre-operative encouragement and instruction at a personal level lessened the need for analgesia following surgery. Another study by Skipper and Leonard (1968) found that supportive interaction by professional carers reduced stress in mothers following illness in their children. Beecher (1955, 1961) in studying the placebo response noted that up to a third of the success of any intervention may be attributed to the patients' belief that something was being done. Balint (1957) too was clear that paying attention to communication meant that more effective care could take place. Is it perhaps the case that the rapid advance of technology in health care led to this vital component being put to one side?

Central to the idea of reflective practice is a consideration of the professional's self, the unique person of the practitioner. Rather than being a neutral and objective agent, the health professional is seen as central to the work of healing. As Yalom notes, 'the effective therapist cannot remain detached, passive and hidden' (Yalom, 1980, p.411).

The use of self in therapeutic practice involves the development of clinical wisdom. Whilst clinical wisdom may start with theories and models, it moves far beyond these

> ...to encompass a rich, potent and varied blend of life experience, self awareness, technical and procedural expertise, ethical judgement and perspicacity, together with a sound understanding of one's own limits of knowledge and competence. (Wosket 1999, p.29)

The advantages of reflective practice are several. For example, with a greater degree of awareness, practitioners can have a clearer idea of the various sources of strain and stress they are experiencing and be able to do something to prevent it from interfering with the care being offered. Practitioners can also look at their knowledge and skills and identify shortfalls. Very importantly, they can also become aware of counter-transference issues.

The idea of counter-transference has a long history going back to Sigmund Freud (1933). It is a process whereby thoughts and feelings are stimulated in the healer as a result of the work being done. Two forms of counter-transference have been identified (Clarkson 1995). The pro-active form consists of those feelings which are brought into clinical situations from the professional's own history. For example, a nurse is providing support to a woman whose mother has just died. Without warning the nurse suddenly feels overwhelmed by feelings of intense sadness and finds it hard to prevent tears from flowing. She stops listening to her client and begins to panic. It was only later and with the help of the ward sister that the nurse realised that she was remembering the death of her own mother when she was ten. Thus an aspect of a patient's biography may without warning stimulate a memory of a painful event in the professional's own life. For a while the professional may be incapacitated by the clarity of the memory and the intensity of the associated feelings.

The other kind of counter-transference is called reactive. In this case what the therapist is feeling is being stimulated directly by the patient. For example, a client is describing something terrible that happened to him some years ago. The client shows absolutely no sign of emotion. After a few minutes of hearing this story, the practitioner begins to experience feelings of sadness. These feelings may indicate the true impact of the event in the client's life even though the client is unable, as yet, to recognise the emotional pain associated with the memory because he is so strongly defended.

The journey to insight

The development of awareness is a key element in what occurs in the process of reflective practice. Practitioners begin to recognise that their own psychological processes, including the ones they would prefer to remain hidden, may sometimes be a liability but perhaps may also be an asset. Trying to disentangle healing impairments from healing benefits is an ongoing struggle. The longest journey made, and the hardest, may be the journey into self. But I believe that it is an essential exercise for anyone engaged in therapeutic practice to reflect deeply, carefully and frequently on the links between their own psychological characteristics and attributes, their personal experience and their professional activities. Practitioners need to have sufficiently resolved their own issues not to have kept parts of themselves away from transactions with clients or shut parts of themselves down because they cannot bear to have them re-stimulated. As Wosket (1999) notes, 'the measure of my effectiveness is how much I can bear to be touched. If I need to duck, dodge, dive I will be blocking the work needed' (pp.32–33).

People in professions dedicated to care can better empathise with clients' situations if they have examined, come to terms with, and attained a degree of understanding of their own values, feelings and previous relevant experience. I give a few examples to illustrate.

When I was a child I often felt blamed for things that I knew I had not done. Today when I am with clients, I am particularly sensitive to their sense of injustice and am able to give them a sense of being understood which they describe as liberating. Another example; I learned as a child to appreciate and to become very involved in a good story. Now I am adept at remembering even small details of clients' stories, which although they may appear to be insignificant, can be developed therapeutically. Finally, I loved listening to the radio from an early age. Today I am aware that I am skilled in listening. There is much to be harnessed from our own unique blend of experience and I give these examples to show the way so much of what might be considered unimportant can be brought into healing work.

The wounded healer

At least part of what I have been writing about above relates to the notion of the 'wounded healer', well exemplified by Michael Kearney (1996). The idea of the wounded healer is based on the extremely old myth of Chiron. He was born a centaur with a human head and torso and the body of a horse and because of his parentage he was half mortal and half immortal. Chiron was adopted by the sun god, Apollo, who brought him up to be wise and knowledgeable. One day Chiron was attending a feast. He was accidentally hit and seriously wounded in the knee by a poisoned arrow. Because he was half immortal Chiron did not die but was left with an agonising wound. He withdrew to a mountain retreat and began to search for relief from his suffering, a search that continued for the rest of his life. Although unable to cure himself, he discovered many healing remedies for others. He became renowned for the compassion he showed and the healing and comfort he brought to his many visitors. His ability to heal others was directly linked to having journeyed in depth into his own wounded self (Kearney 1996, p.42).

The idea of the wounded healer is not just a myth, and in the biographies of many people who have dedicated their lives to caring for others, there will be a history of experience of illness, pain, depression, loss and despair in self or in someone close. Indeed, many healers choose their profession in response to their own experience of being a client, and ongoing healing becomes a significant motivating factor for the work they do. Hycner (1991, p.12) wrote that 'it is the very nature of one's own difficulties which sensitise the therapist to the vulnerability of the other'. Alice Miller too has suggested that many psychotherapists suffer a form of emotional disturbance arising from the experience of unmet needs in childhood. However, it is precisely this experience that nourishes therapeutic abilities. 'The therapist's sensitivities, empathetic responsiveness and powerful antennae indicate that as a child he probably used to fulfil other people's needs and repress his own' (Miller 1997, p.22).

The fact that in the process of their work, practitioners' own need for healing can be satisfied does not lessen the importance of using the whole self in practice. As Carl Rogers, the founder of the person-centred movement, wrote: 'I think it's helpful to start with the basic, but true, premise that real service does not happen unless both people are being served' (Rogers 1967, p.18). Rogers is highlighting the reciprocity involved in the healing process. Likewise Carl Jung and his followers describe a relevant archetype:

> The healer and the patient are two aspects of the same. When a person becomes sick, the healer-patient archetype is constellated. The sick man seeks an external healer, but at the same time the intra psychic healer is activated... But what about the physician? Here we encounter the archetype of the wounded healer. The doctor's empathy is made available to the patient by the doctor's connection with his or her own vulnerability, when this is not blocked by the denial which comes, amongst other things, from fear of being emotionally overwhelmed or systematically unsupported. (Guggenbuhl-Craig 1971)

And as Miller and Baldwin (1987, p.149) wrote:

> Denial and repression of one's brokenness and vulnerability by itself may rob a healer of psychic energy and contribute to burnout. The act of affirming common human brokenness and vulnerability can bring life giving energy and healing to both healer and patient.

Everyone has suffered in some way. What is being suggested here is that the experience of suffering can, if fully integrated into the self, enable practitioners to be more effective healers of others. We can gain in wisdom from the experience of suffering.

Dealing with the wounds arising from professional practice

So far I have been dealing with the 'wounds' that the healer brings into professional practice but the other side of this is concerned with the wounds that occur as a result of the practice itself. Every day those in the caring professions will encounter situations of disease, distress, disablement: people who are broken-hearted, anxious, depressed. How are they to respond?

> For that element of tragedy which lies in the very fact of frequency has not yet wrought itself into the coarse emotion of mankind; and perhaps our frames could hardly bear much of it. If we had a keen vision and feeling of ordinary life, it would be like hearing the grass grow and the squirrel's heart beat and we should die of the roar that lies on the other side of silence. (Eliot 1871–1872)

One of the most common experiences in health care practice is the experience of loss and disappointment. Yet most of this loss remains unacknowledged. Practitioners rarely fully grieve the losses experienced in their work. This is partly because in the West so many of us have been brought up without the awareness that grieving loss is important for psychological health. How often is it the case that as children the beloved pet that dies is replaced by another without the one who has died being mourned?

Remen (1996) tells the story of going to a library just before she began a new post and looking for books on death. She found that there were few. She suggests that the amount of space given to death in the library echoed the amount given in her own consciousness. Remen had been working as a paediatrician and during that time many of the children she had cared for had died. She had grieved for none of these children. Many years later she began to experience a series of dreams, disturbing in their content. With help she began to realise that the very real care and concern she had felt for these children and the great sadness when they had died, had never been acknowledged.

As Remen (1996) notes: 'the expectation that we can be immersed in suffering and loss daily and not be touched by it is as unrealistic as expecting to be able to walk through water without getting wet' (p.52). The way we deal with loss can shape our capacity to be present in life and be present to clients in their pain. Remen suggests that protecting ourselves from loss rather than grieving and healing our losses is one of the most important causes of burnout. Lest I am misunderstood, I am not advocating a particular form of grief journey that is essential to travel. I am not suggesting that moving through the 'tasks of grief' (Worden 1991) is an essential part of the healing process. What I do advocate, however, is that in whatever way is personally and culturally appropriate, time is taken to recall the people who have been our patients and the way we think and feel about them. The work is emotionally costly and sometimes very difficult indeed and I believe that it is important to remember this. Maybe all that will be needed is to speak with a colleague. But sometimes clients will impact on us at a very deep level. On occasions such as these, professional supervision or techniques like creative writing can be very helpful.

Using the self in healing

I have been arguing that one of the very important aspects of healing, whatever the location or context in which it takes place, is the way in which the self of the practitioner is brought into the process. There are many different ways in which this can happen. Here I identify five.

1. Listening

I suspect that the most basic and powerful way to connect to another person is to listen fully and deeply to what he or she is saying. In the process of listening, attention is given fully to the other. It sounds so simple. But it is also remarkable. So many patients say that they have been attended to for the very first time in their lives and that they leave a consultation feeling much better in themselves as a result. Listening is the oldest and perhaps the most powerful tool of healing. It is often through the quality of our listening and not the wisdom of our words that we are able to effect the most profound changes in the people around us. Listening without judgement affirms the validity of the other. Listening gives the opportunity for the development of wholeness. As Remen (1996) notes: 'when you listen generously to people, they can hear truth in themselves, often for the first time' (p.220).

But although it sounds so basic and unproblematic, listening is a demanding skill especially when the risk is taken to allow clients to touch the tender places and vulnerabilities of the professional's self.

2. Sharing our humanity

Carl Rogers (1961) is said to have taken time before every session to remember his humanity – to remember that, above all else, he was a human being like each and every one of the people who came to him for help. I sometimes wonder how hard we work at trying to get away from our humanity. I know that I have tried very hard indeed to acquire knowledge, to develop expertise in various spheres of work, to look at what I need to cultivate to be an effective practitioner. Winnicott (1965) coined the phrase 'good enough' in relation to parenting. But in the high-aspiring world of the twenty-first century, how many of us can accept such a standard. I certainly became convinced that it was not enough to be 'good enough' and tried to make myself other than I am. It took me a long time to learn that in healing work, it is hard to trust someone with your vulnerability unless you can see in him or her a matching vulnerability. 'In some basic way it is our imperfections and even our pain that draws others close to us' and provides a place for safety, security and healing (Remen 1996, p.113).

3. Living with uncertainty and mystery

Casement (1985) writes that one of the losses involved in training is that it is possible to become deaf to the unexpected and blind to what is different and strange. This can come about because in training we learn about theories, of causation, of cure, and of much else. There is nothing wrong with theories as such, provided they are seen for what they are – provisional explanations, a way of structuring complex data, tools to help us manage in difficult situations, ways of structuring the world so that we are saved from the anxiety attendant on a feeling that all is chaos. In working with people in distress, if we are able to resist the desire for order and coherence, to fit what is being said into a category of the known, and to allow the strangeness and newness of *this* person's unique experience to occupy our attention, we can perhaps deal more ably with the immediacy and reality of this person's unhappiness, perplexity or fear (Campbell 1981, p.105).

For myself, I have become more relaxed in my desire for structure and have learned to live with how little I know or understand. There is nothing quite like working with people who are dying to take me to the edge of certainty. I am now comfortable to work with mystery, to wait for the unspoken to emerge, to work with image and metaphor, and to let the story be told by the speaker at his or her own pace.

4. The power of love

Many practitioners are taught during their training that it is necessary to be objective in working with people, and the ideas of Sir William Osler (1892) are used to support this contention. He is said to have advised objectivity. However, as Remen (1996, p.79) points out, the word 'objectivity' is a rather poor translation of the Latin word used by Osler, which was *aequanimatas*. This is much better translated as 'calmness of mind' or 'inner peace' and has nothing to do with objectivity or the sense of emotional distance that is associated with the word.

Rather than objectivity, I would suggest that engagement and involvement are the aspects of relationship that are important in healing. I would even venture further and suggest that love plays a significant part in healing! Here I am referring to the kind of unconditional love which demands nothing in return and wants only the growth and fulfilment of the loved one. It is a strengthening love, a love that, by definition, does not burden or obligate the loved one (Kahn 1997, p.39). It is 'the ability to care deeply enough about the other person to commit myself fully and unconditionally to their process of change and development without requiring anything myself that might diminish the other person in return' (Wosket 1999, p.41). Holeson (1985, p.280) equates love with tenderness, and says that 'without tenderness the noise of our talk does harm'. The majority of professionals are afraid of speaking about the love which may be operating in their work, and equate it with an absence of professionalism, being over-involved, and so on. It may then be described as something else as, for example, in the case of Carl Rogers (1967), who appeared to call what I name as love 'unconditional positive regard'. Remen (1996) became aware of the power of love but not until much later in her career. She writes 'I had carried the belief that as a physician my love didn't matter and the only thing of value I had to offer was my knowledge and skill… Medicine is as close to love as it is to science, and its relationships matter even at the edge of life itself' (p.65).

5. The power of stories

We are all unique and it is our uniqueness that gives us value and meaning. Yet we also yearn for connection and ways to transcend the isolation that separates us from each other and from ourselves. Telling stories and listening to each other's stories, we learn what makes us similar and what connects us all. Listening to the stories of the clients with whom I work, I discover the heroism of ordinary people living ordinary lives.

For the next nine chapters, people who have worked in the healing professions tell their stories. All of them have been on a journey, have learned the value of self-discovery and of bringing their unique selves into their work in a way which profoundly enriches their professional lives but more importantly, the lives of people who suffer. It is to these people that I now give over these pages.

References

Balint, M. (1957) *The Doctor His Patient and the Illness.* London: Tavistock.

Beecher, H. (1955) 'The Powerful Placebo.' *Journal of the American Medical Association 159*, 602.

Beecher, H. (1961) 'Surgery as Placebo.' *Journal of the American Medical Association 176*, 1102.

Bloom, S. (1963) *The Doctor and his Patient: A Sociological Interpretation.* New York: Russell Sage Foundation.

Byrne, P. and Long, B. (1976) *Doctors Talking to Patients.* London: Her Majesty's Stationery Office.

Campbell, A. (1981) *Rediscovering Palliative Care.* London: Darton Longman and Todd.

Casement, P. (1985) *On Learning from the Patient.* London: Routledge.

Chadwick, J. and Mann, W. (1950) *Hippocratic Writings.* Middlesex: Penguin.

Clarkson, P. (1995) The *Therapeutic Relationship.* London: Whurr.

Duff, R. and Hollingshead, A. (1968) *Sickness and Society.* London: Harper and Row.

Egbert, J. (1964) 'Reduction in post-operative pain by encouragement and instruction of patients.' *New England Journal of Medicine 270*, 825.

Eliot, G. (1871–2) *Middlemarch* (first published in instalments). London: Penguin Books.

Field, D. (1976) 'The Social Definition of Illness.' In D. Tuckett (ed) *An Introduction to Medical Sociology*. London: Tavistock.

Fletcher, C. (1973) *The Rock Carling Fellowship Monograph 1972: Communication in Medicine*. London: Nuffield Provincial Hospitals Trust.

Freidson, E. (1961) *Patients' Views of Medical Practice*. New York: Russell Sage Foundation.

Freud, S. (1933) *New Introductory Lectures on Psycho-analyses*. London: Harmondsworth.

Frost, C. and King, N. (2000) 'Physician heal thyself: the emotional demands of general practice.' Proceedings of the British Psychological Society's Occupational Psychology Conference. Brighton.

General Medical Council (1993) 'Tomorrow's Doctors: Recommendations on Undergraduate Medical Education.' London: General Medical Council.

Guggenbuhl-Craig, A. (1971) *Power in the Helping Professions*. Texas: Spring.

Holeson, R. (1985) *Forms of Feeling: The Heart of Psychotherapy*. London: Routledge.

Holohan, A. (1977) 'Diagnosis: The end of transition.' In A. Davis and G. Horobin (eds) *Medical Encounters: The Experience of Illness and Treatment*. London: Croom Helm.

Hunter, W. (c.1780) 'Introductory Lectures to Students.' St Thomas' Hospital Manuscript 55, 182.

Hurwitz, B. (2000) 'Narrative and the practice of medicine.' *The Lancet 356*, 9247, 2086–9.

Hycner, R. (1991) *Between Person and Person: Towards a Dialogical Psychotherapy*. New York: The Gestalt Journal.

Kahn, M. (1997) *Between Therapist and Client: The New Relationship*. New York: Freeman.

Kearney, M. (1996) *Mortally Wounded*. Dublin: Marino Books.

Kirklin, D. and Richardson, R. (eds) (2001) *Medical Humanities: A Practical Introduction*. London: Royal College of Physicians.

Mason, C. (1984) 'Studies in Medical Care.' University of Dundee: Ph.D. Thesis.

Merrison Committee (1975) *Report of the Committee of Inquiry into the Regulation of the Medical Profession*. London: Her Majesty's Stationery Office.

Metcalfe, D. (1983) 'The mismatch between undergraduate education and the medical task.' In D. Pendleton and J. Hasler (eds) *Doctor Patient Communication*. London: Academic Press.

Miller, A. (1997) The *Drama of Being a Child: The Search for the True Self.* London: Virago.

Miller, G. and Baldwin, D. Jr (1987) 'Implications of the wounded-healer paradigm for the use of self in therapy.' In M. Baldwin and V. Satir (eds) *The Use of Self.* New York: Haworth Press.

Murray, R. (1983) 'The mentally ill doctor.' *Practitioner 227,* 65.

Osler, W. (1892) *The Principles and Practice of Medicine.* New York: Apleton.

Pendleton, D. and Hasler, J. (eds) (1983) *Doctor Patient Communication.* London: Academic Press.

Petrone, M. (ed) (1999) *Touching the Rainbow: Pictures and Words by People Affected by Cancer.* Brighton: East Sussex Brighton and Hove Health Authority.

Petrone, M. (2001) 'The healing touch: the necessity for humanity in medicine and the humanities in medical education.' In D. Kirklin and R. Richardson (eds) *Medical Humanities: A practical introduction.* London: The Royal College of Physicians, 32.

Remen, R. (1996) *Kitchen Table Wisdom.* New York: Riverhead Books.

Rogers, C. (1961) *On Becoming a Person.* Boston: Houghton Mifflin.

Rogers, C. (1967) *On Becoming a Person: A Therapist's View of Psychotherapy.* London: Constable.

Schon, D. (1983) *The Reflective Practitioner: How Practitioners Think in Practice.* New York: Basic Books.

Schon, D. (1987) *Educating the Reflective Practitioner: Towards a New Design for Teaching and Learning in the Professions.* San Francisco: Josey Bass.

Skipper, J. and Leonard, R. (1968) 'Children, stress and hospitalisation: a field experiment.' *Journal of Health and Human Behaviour 9,* 275.

Strong, P. (1977) 'Medical Errands: A discussion of routine medical work.' In A. Davis and G. Horobin (eds) *Medical Encounters: The Experience of Illness and Treatment.* London: Croom Helm.

Tate, P. (1983) 'Doctor's Style.' In D. Pendleton and J. Hasler (eds) *Doctor Patient Communication.* London: Academic Press.

Twycross, R. (1975) *The Dying Patient.* London: Christian Medical Fellowship.

Weatherall, D. (1994) 'The inhumanity of medicine.' *British Medical Journal 309,* 1671–1672.

Winnicott, D. (1965) *The Family and Individual Development.* London: Tavistock.

Worden, W. (1991) *Grief Counselling and Grief Therapy*. London: Routledge.

Wosket, V. (1999) *The Therapeutic Use of the Self*. London: Routledge.

Yalom, I. (1980) *Existential Psychotherapy*. New York: Basic Books.

2

Medicine and Palliative Care

The Bronze Serpent

Louis Heyse-Moore

I hear and behold God in every object, yet understand God not in the
least...
(Whitman 1960a, p.442)

An accidental happening

When I was five years old, I was playing in the street of the village
where we lived and I came across a man surrounded by a crowd. He
had been hit by a car, and sat propped against a wall with a blanket
around him; his dark hair contrasted with his pale, shocked face.
The people around him were staring with a sort of horrified
fascination, as did I. This was no idle moment spent gossiping; what
had happened engaged us all and touched us in the marrow of our
bones. We were looking at the possibility of death while secretly
relieved that it was not for us. This must have been how it was when
a crowd attended a hanging in past centuries. And yet there was
compassion here too; he had been helped off the road and someone
had fetched a blanket for him, while a policeman stood guard.

Breathing

At about the same age I developed asthma, perhaps as a result of
moving to a new house and new allergic possibilities. I would wake
at around 4 am, acutely short of breath, each respiration a huge
effort. Outside my window there was a grey darkness and I longed

for the first glimmer of dawn. I tried, as best I could, to calm myself by breathing slowly and deeply and as economically as possible. I would focus on each in-breath and then each long, wheezing out-breath, a sort of desperate meditation.

He was the most breathless patient I have ever looked after in all my years of working in palliative medicine. Cancer had run riot through his lungs and death was imminent. His skin was a greyish-blue colour from lack of oxygen and he shifted jerkily like a bird trying to find the position of least agony, while he gasped ceaselessly. Sometimes he would lean over his bed-table, sometimes he would prop himself up on his arms trying to stretch his chest out. Urgent action was needed. I gave him an intravenous injection of a tranquilliser and watched him gradually subside into sleep, though even then his chest still heaved as if it had a life of its own. He died the next day. I was glad to have relieved his distress, though sobered by the depth of his ordeal.

Shadows

Since I was young, depression has been a regular visitor, my faithful shadow as it were. There were, to be sure, many times when the sun shone steadily in my inner world, but always the hated, yet comfortably familiar, darkness returned, ineluctable and pursuing me with exactly the same strength of will with which I fled it.

At first, its ministrations seemed gentle and even beautiful: crepuscular sadness, reverie, curling up in bed or wanting to be alone. But, little by little, it grew, so subtly that I hardly noticed, and it began to oppress me and be painful, like a heavy stone placed on one's chest is painful. It became like an attack, a dark beast waiting invisibly in the shadows to pounce and bear me down. Then, all I could do was roll figuratively into a hedgehog ball, arms around my knees and head tucked down, waiting stubbornly for the storm to pass.

As I think back on my work, there seem to be many such people, speaking the same words. They were dying; they were a burden on their family; there was no point in living any more; the pain was unbearable; they wanted to end it all. I was faced with the psyche's pain at the prospect of dying, and depression was one of its manifestations. I discovered a dissonant resonance with my own times of depression. I noticed particularly how there seemed to be a wall that the ill had set up between themselves and the world; a grey, smooth, cold, stone wall, hard to break down. They only had weeks to live; how could I help someone in that short space of time?

Gradually, I came to realise that *every* part of the patient – body, mind, relationships and spirit – had to be taken into account; whole-person care in other words. Remove only the presenting aspect of the distress and, Hydra-like, it would reappear somewhere else. Psychological pain might transmute into physical pain, erupt as family conflict or take the form of self-destructive behaviour such as alcoholism. The American psychotherapist Paula Reeves (1999, p.xi) comments in this context: 'When we neglect what matters most to us, that then becomes the matter with us,' neatly pointing to how the cause of psychological and other illnesses is so often the place of healing too.

Immediately, then, it becomes obvious that different disciplines need to work together to confront such pain effectively. I remember one woman, a young, immigrant, single mother with a secondary brain cancer, who, in addition to medical and nursing input, was also seen by the physiotherapist, social worker, counsellor, chaplain, aromatherapist and art therapist, not to mention her friends and family. Whenever I went to see her medically, I was aware of how extraordinarily rapidly she was processing psychologically what was happening to her, her fears about her illness and impending death, and her anxieties about how her daughter would manage without her. The network of professionals from different disciplines who worked with her acted as a creative container that facilitated her coming to terms with her life's end.

This web of support was professional and skilled, of course, but there was something more going on: one could call it care, perhaps, or compassion. It involved, also, respect and a sense of concern. The language of poetry may say it better, as in the poem 'Love (111)' by George Herbert (1996, p.123):

Love bade me welcome; yet my soul drew back,
Guilty of dust and sin.
But quick-eyed love, observing me grow slack
From my first entrance in,
Drew nearer to me, sweetly questioning
If I lack'd anything.

Stille Nacht

One adolescent night, I sat watching the flickering fire and listening to a record of Schubert's Impromptus. I entered a state of stillness in which, without effort, I heard every note of the music like drops of water falling on a calm lake. No thoughts; no time.

She was anxious, short of breath and tense; she had lung cancer. I taught her a simple muscle relaxation exercise. Before my eyes, I saw her body begin to soften and melt and her breathing to slow. She allowed herself to be supported by her bed and volunteered that she felt wonderful. Afterwards, it was as though she had been transformed, and she remained peaceful until she died two days later. I was amazed by how such a simple intervention had such a profound effect. I wished it were always like that. In truth, though, such serendipitous events can't be planned in advance. Instead, each encounter has the potential to be a journey into the unknown, one that may involve shadow as well as light, pain as well as healing, conflict as well as peace. How often do we dare to take such risks?

Pictures at an exhibition

Throughout my childhood, I was an avid reader of myths, fairy tales, legends, adventures and fantasies. A whole gallery of characters was at my disposal and their images spoke to me in myriad ways: the compassionate Doctor Dolittle, who could talk with animals; Tumnus, the faun in *The Lion, the Witch and the Wardrobe*, good-hearted but forced into betraying Lucy; Odysseus, the wily survivor; Medusa, epitome of the dark feminine, whose serpent-framed face turned people to stone; the elusive and magical Firebird, a bright flame in the endless, dark, Russian forests; the children of Lir, doomed by an enchantment to take the form of swans for 900 years; and so many others.

And there were the places too: the garden of the Hesperides; the blessed isles of Avalon; dark Hades; the stormy straits between Scylla and Charybdis; Eden in all its innocence.

Even the hated, back-aching, feet-hurting, childhood visits to art galleries served a purpose here. My memory would store away some picture that meant little at the time, but was like a seed that germinated, sometimes decades later. Later, as an adult, I came to realise that these images were powerful partly because they represented visually the invisible archetypes, or foundation stones of the psyche, described by Carl Jung (1964). They were like dreams, and, like dreams, they often had a message. Images that rose unbidden to my mind during the day were not necessarily mental detritus but might actually possess a wisdom, an echo of the divine, if one could but find the key.

On admission to the hospice, she was very agitated. Not surprising, one might think, considering she had cerebral metastases from a primary breast cancer. However, talking to her, the diagnosis was not quite so straightforward. She had good reason to be anxious: her husband refused to talk about her illness and she had two young children. In addition, she had been through a gruelling series of treatments, culminating in brain radiotherapy. Having got to know her, I suggested a visualisation exercise in which she was invited to imagine a calm lake on a sunny day, the sights, sounds, smells, tastes and feel of the place. As she did this, her hyper-alert restless state was gradually replaced by stillness and calm. She was delighted and this signalled a change in her. Now she felt more able to talk about herself, to try to prepare her children for her impending death and to reach out to her silent husband. In a further visualisation exercise, she imagined meeting someone by the lake, someone wise who could help her. It turned out to be her mother who had died a while before. She found the experience very profound. It was not that her mother had any miraculous solutions, rather that she was supportive and loving to her sick daughter, who desperately needed help. And as for me, I felt moved by this young woman's courage and respectful of her inner strength. I felt, as I often do in such circumstances, that we met, not just as doctor and patient, but as one human being face to face with another. And I felt as well a protest within me; surely this was one person whose time should not have come yet. What of her children? What of her husband? What of her, young as she was?

Secrets

Lying never came easy to me.

I had just qualified and was working as a house surgeon. I was clerking in a patient who had come in for surgery on a thyroid cancer. Unusually, she had had two other different, primary cancers in the past, both cured by surgery. I had practised my share of evasions and silences designed to prevent patients asking me what was wrong with them, but that day I felt angry at a system of medicine that encouraged such deception. So, I didn't try and dodge. Suddenly she asked me if the cancer had come back again. My pulse rate trebled and I could feel my heart thudding in my throat. I had never told anyone they had cancer but I couldn't find it in me to lie and so I said quietly, 'Yes'.

She began to cry: 'Why does it keep coming back?' she said, and I could only sit with her; I don't recall my reply. Probably the words weren't important. Just the human contact was what was needed; person-to-person again.

Surgery

When I pass by a ruined cottage or barn in the country, suffused with a soft and haunting nostalgia, I sometimes find myself thinking how I'd like to rebuild it, make it whole again.

As a medical student I used to watch my father, a surgeon, operating. This was his world, where he was master and in his element. The scene had something of the air of a sacred rite: the green vestments, the strange hats and face masks, the lighting subdued except for the shaft of brilliant light focused on the operation and the voices quiet and concentrated. In his hand, his right hand, was the scalpel that was like the proverbial two-edged sword – it could kill and it could cure. It seemed miraculous that the patients, in a death-like sleep, could survive a huge gash in their abdomen and hands delving deep among their bowels. And yet they did.

In psychotherapy, working with my depressions, I discovered a truth which is beautifully expressed in this excerpt from the Exodus story, when the Israelites wandered in the wilderness for forty years:

> God sent fiery serpents among the people; their bite brought death to many in Israel. The people came and said to Moses, 'We have sinned by speaking against Yahweh and against you. Intercede with Yahweh to save us from these serpents.' Moses interceded for the people, and Yahweh answered him, 'Make a fiery serpent and put it on a standard. If anyone is bitten and looks at it, he shall live.' So Moses fashioned a bronze serpent which he put on a standard, and if anyone was bitten by a serpent, he looked at the bronze serpent and lived. (Numbers 21:6–9)

What this is saying, I think, is that when we are in crisis, it is the act of facing the pain, hard though it may be, which can bring resolution and healing. In a way, the therapist becomes the bronze serpent on the standard reflecting this image back to the client. But, to do this means a journey into the unknown psyche, which is like an operation: a search through the entrails of the mind to discover the roots of the sickness.

And I found, similarly, that this was precisely how I worked with some patients, those who wished to follow this path. I had always felt a gap between my medical specialisation and that of my father; here, then, was an unexpected bridge, a conjunction of opposites.

Flight of the spirit

I love watching birds. Two particular memories, two of many, come to mind:

Down by the sea, near where I lived, the gulls would soar for hours, their brilliant white wings gleaming against the blue sky as they side-slipped down and then climbed up the invisible air currents. I liked to look at them and always associate them with the sharp smell of salt water, of beaches, precipitous cliffs and the sound of waves. They reminded me of something the poet Robert Bridges (1960, p.480) wrote about in his poem 'Nightingales':

> Beautiful must be the mountains whence ye come,
> And bright in the fruitful valleys the streams wherefrom
> Ye learn your song:
> Where are those starry woods? O might I wander there,
> Among the flowers, which in that heavenly air
> Bloom the year long!

Once, too, when I was visiting Antwerp Zoo, in the tropical aviary I came across a bird of paradise, resplendent in its plumage of iridescent velvet green, gold, and long, gauzy tail-feathers that shimmered like a cloud as it moved around. Its very name spoke of mystery, a rare and secretive creature that came from the inaccessible rain forests of New Guinea on the other side of the world. It was like that Firebird of Russian legend which was endowed with supernatural powers.

Birds, then, remind me of the spiritual world of light and air, and, too, the realm of the soul, rich, sensual and golden.

It might be supposed that patients who are dying would spend much of their time distressed, whether sad or frightened, angry or depressed, and it's true that these feelings do occur; but not all the time. An example (Heyse-Moore 1996, pp.297–315) will give a flavour of what I mean:

> 'One woman…described waking in the middle of the night in a darkened palliative care ward where two other patients were close to death. She suddenly experienced lights very brightly, far above her; she looked around but there seemed to be no-one there and everything was silent; this she found extremely beautiful and peaceful and she thought she was dying and in heaven. This experience was for her profoundly moving and reassuring and she recounted it the next day with complete lucidity.

There are hundreds of written accounts of spiritual experiences in the dying. They occur in people of every religious tradition and in those of none (James 1977), and they happen in people who are manifestly sane.

There is, too, a delightful and liberating inclusiveness about them that cuts across spiritual racism.

I wonder, too, about those with the altered mental states we call psychoses, delirium or acute confusion. Can we be so sure that their hallucinations and delusions are *always* just the product of a sick mind? I've talked to many patients who report seeing dead relatives or friends and some who have reported near death experiences in the past. I may not be able to see what they see, but does that always mean there is nothing there? To me, the dying would be the very people most likely to be aware of different realities.

The wounded healer

Here's a story I always find moving – the myth of Chiron the centaur.

Chiron, half horse and half man, was an orphan who was found, brought up and taught by Apollo. He became tutor to Hercules, Jason and especially Asklepios, the mythical founder of western medicine. He was at a wedding feast when his drunken kin rioted. Hercules came to quell the disturbance and accidently shot Chiron through the leg with a poisoned arrow. The poison was deadly, but Chiron could not die as he was immortal. In agony he searched for a cure. Although he could not find one, he became expert in the many medicines he tried and so became a renowned healer to whom the poor turned for help. Hercules pleaded with Zeus and Chiron was allowed to become mortal by exchanging places with Prometheus, who had stolen fire from the gods. Chiron descended into Hades, but Zeus took pity on him and raised him to immortality and a place among the constellations of the stars.

This is a complex story, but I would like to pick out two themes from it. One is about the orphaned child Chiron, half horse and half man, surely a monstrous creature, a freak, fit only for ridicule! But, if we think a little further, something different emerges. Horses are very much part of the natural world and so remind us of our own bodies, of our own physical nature, of our needs, our feelings, our desires. I used to ride when I was young and I remember the intoxication of galloping at full tilt, almost flying, afraid but excited, myself and the horse as one.

And then there is the human element, the star-gazer. As Hamlet so famously puts it: 'What a piece of work is man! How noble in reason! how infinite in faculty!...in action how like an angel! in apprehension how like a god!' (Craig 1905)

But imagine one aspect without the other! We would be left either with an instinctual animal or with a disembodied dreamer. No, Chiron's story reminds us we are both – body and soul – and both are important. Where could the soul live in the world but in a body? And what would the body be without a soul?

The second aspect of this story is Chiron's illness. It seems cruelly unfair that someone so manifestly not evil should have to suffer in this way. This is the 'Why me?' question so often asked. Certainly this has been a question for me when I have been depressed and looking for cures and, even more certainly, what I have learnt has been invaluable in my work with dying people. Would I have gained this knowledge without my experiences of depression? Almost certainly not. Has it been worth it? I think so, despite the pain; but this is a dangerous sort of knowledge bought at a cost – which makes it all the more precious I suppose.

Here, then, we are confronted with a paradox: that the person who heals has himself or herself been wounded. This seems strange and contrary to reason; surely the healer should be healthy? However, I can recall from my own experience a cardiologist with heart disease, a rheumatologist with a limp, a palliative care physician with cancer and a psychiatrist with depression, among many others. There is a curious link here, because this is the experience of healers or shamans in traditional societies. They, too, would often undergo some major psychological or physical illness, a perilous initiation which might even bring them to the point of death before they recovered to take up their calling. The world religions contain a plethora of examples: St Francis, apart from his well-known stigmata echoing the crucifixion of Christ, suffered from severe eye infections such that he was almost blind at the end of his life. Mohammed was persecuted for promulgating his angelic visions. The Buddha knowingly died of food poisoning. It would seem, then, that it is our very ills that drive us to search, not only for our own healing, but that of others too.

And yet, this is the very thing that we strive to hide from the world. We must always be caring, strong, competent and untiring. If, though, you were to look into the mind of any doctor, you would find the same array of suffering as is the lot of the rest of the world: bereavements, childhood traumas, separations, loneliness, illness and so on. In one way or another we are all wounded, whatever our outward appearance may be. In support of this point, a study by Finlay (1990, pp.5–9) showed high levels of stress-related symptoms such as insomnia, depersonalisation and suicidal thoughts among hospice medical directors and matrons.

The wild card

> It appears so easy in the Gospels. Jesus has only to spend a couple of minutes with a sick person and he is healed. The dumb man talks, Lazarus is raised from the dead, the blind man sees and the demoniac is exorcised.

It seemed like a straightforward palliative care referral: a woman with a primary liver cancer confirmed by biopsy, and spread to the lungs demonstrated on chest X-ray. She was past any treatment and would die soon. But when I went to visit her at home, she seemed too well for someone with advanced cancer. And when I examined her abdomen, the liver, which had been reported as grossly enlarged from the cancer, was now only just palpable. Somehow it had shrunk dramatically. She was too well to need my help so I suggested to her general practitioner that the investigations be repeated. The chest X-ray showed that the lung spread had disappeared and abdominal scans that the liver tumour had indeed decreased markedly. Follow-up scans showed that it continued to diminish, and a final liver biopsy showed only scar tissue with no evidence of cancer. I visited her again a year later and she was in good health.

What was this? A spontaneous remission? Of course it was, in the sense that it was spontaneous and the cancer remitted. But that tells us very little. Was it a miracle? Certainly she was a very devout Christian and she and her family had prayed every day for a cure. She remembered waking up one day with a very strong feeling that everything would be all right, and improved from then on.

Whenever I tell this story to other doctors, I usually find a polite interest and then a moving on to a different subject. I am surprised at this, since here is such an extraordinary story. Surely, it seems to me, if this is a natural phenomenon, wouldn't a better understanding of it have dramatic implications for the treatment of cancer? And if this is a supernatural event, what does this say to all those who do not believe in the supernatural? Maybe it's because this story is like a wild card, it doesn't fit into any conventional slots, so its easier to forget about it. If we don't forget, we may be forced to change our minds, and who wants to do that?

But what about this case? Another patient, who also had liver cancer, but secondary this time. When she came into the hospice, she was smiling broadly and even laughing. She, too, had a deep faith in God and she knew that he was going to heal her. When I examined her, the monstrous cancer filled half her abdomen. Her Pentecostal church supported her strongly through their prayers and the visits of her pastor – they, too, felt she would be cured. Over the weeks, the expected miracle did not occur and I watched her slowly weakening while the cancer grew even larger. Though she maintained her belief that it would go, she gradually grew quieter and would sometimes talk about other matters. She was in tears as she reflected on the loss of her childhood home. At last she was so weak that all she could do was to say that she was in God's hands, and gradually she slipped into unconsciousness and died. How is it she was not healed? Did she show any less faith? It didn't seem so. Was she less worthy? Not that I knew.

So, we are left with the unknown, mystery – something, I think, beyond intellectual comprehension. Like most people, I don't like not being able to understand, but it seems to me that we must, as best we can, *live* these questions (Rilke 1975), especially when, like it or not, they involve us personally so that we move from the abstract, intellectual plane to a visceral, unfolding, vital experience.

The Dissecting Room

When I began medical school, within the first week we were introduced to the dissecting room, a long rectangle with skylights and rows of tables along each wall like bunks in an army dormitory, each carrying a corpse pickled in formalin and draped with towels and plastic sheeting. There were about eight medical students allocated to dissect each body. The sharp, disagreeable smell of the preservative was everywhere and even permeated our clothes when we left the department.

Early on, we had teaching sessions entitled 'living anatomy'. This meant we all had to appear in the dissecting room in our swimming costumes so that we could study each other's anatomy, in action as it were. This was the stated intent and our teachers stuck to this line. But, how much more was going on unspoken! There were the covert glances as we all sized each other's bodies up. But especially there was the surreal incongruence of a crowd of young, fit medical students walking half-naked around a room full of dead people. It felt, somehow, far more intimate and revealing in this context than on a beach. While we were waiting for our tutors, I sat on a rectangular table with a plastic top. One of the technicians advised me to get off it as there was a body pickling in formalin underneath. I wonder if our teachers had any inkling of what they were asking us to do; or did they think it would help get us used to matters medical? Did they not think that some of the students who were Jewish or Muslim might, for cultural reasons, find this exercise contrary to their custom. Never once in the whole of our time there was the issue of how we might feel about dissecting dead people discussed.

There is a cool beauty about science, about understanding, seeing patterns like the exquisitely elegant double helix structure of DNA and the eureka experience of discovering something no-one else in the world has ever known. But, sometimes, a soullessness can creep in, a coldness of logic, even a deadness. Walt Whitman (1960b, p.439) had this to say:

> When I heard the learn'd astronomer,
> When the proofs, the figures, were ranged in columns before me,
> When I was shown the charts and diagrams, to add, divide, and
> measure them,
> When I sitting heard the astronomer where he lectured with much
> applause in the lecture room,

> How soon unaccountable I became tired and sick,
> Till rising and gliding out I wandered off by myself,
> In the mystical moist night-air, and from time to time,
> Looked up in perfect silence at the stars.

We need also, then, the direct experience of life, tasted, smelt, seen – the mystical moist night-air Whitman writes about – as a counterbalance. To me, cadaver science in that dissecting room drowned out the human stories of both the dead and the living people there. Who were these donors who were generous enough to allow their very bodies to be cut apart? What of their funerals, after the dissections were done? Did anyone attend them, any friend or perhaps a distant relative? Wasn't there something brutal and against nature in carving through another human being's flesh? What about the fear that one might faint or be sick, and so be ridiculed?

I don't wish to be misunderstood here. I know perfectly well that there is a need to learn anatomy and that dissection plays a part. Everyone knows how essential surgery is. It's more about how we approach these and other aspects of medicine, with the whole of ourselves in order that we can treat the whole of the sick person. Medical teaching traditionally goes for objectivity and suppression of feelings and it's no wonder, therefore, that doctors are sometimes accused of being cold and impersonal, and it's no wonder, too, that they have high rates of depression, alcoholism and suicide.

How are the mighty fallen

At one time I was a junior doctor working for a consultant who was famous, eminent and flamboyant; but he didn't tell patients their diagnosis if they had cancer. One day, on a ward round, with a retinue of medical students in tow, he was faced with a patient in his thirties who had a testicular cancer. Many losses threatened here: of manhood, parenthood and even life. Now this patient was persistent. He wanted to know what was wrong and what were his chances of cure, and he wasn't going to be put off by evasive answers. I watched, amazed, as our leader of doctors was reduced to stammering incoherently the information he would never normally give and repeating that no-one is a statistic. It was like watching a balloon deflating. I knew, in fact, that he himself had not long before been diagnosed with a life-threatening illness. What must have been going through his mind! Suddenly, two paradigms had locked horns: the doctor as patriarch, a heroic and invulnerable conqueror of disease and death, versus the doctor as a real person, a fallible human being. Who would you prefer?

Atmosphere

Working in the Special Care Baby Unit was the hardest job I've ever done, involving, as it did, intensive care for premature or very sick babies. When on duty, I'd be up most of the night attending to ventilators and drips in veins the diameter of a thread. But, even though they were newborn, the babies all had personalities. One I remember particularly. She had been born with a fistula or opening between the wind-pipe and gullet. Every time she swallowed any liquid, therefore, it would trickle into her wind-pipe and thence her lungs. She needed immediate surgery to prevent death from pneumonia.

She went off to theatre, and, while I worked on the unit, I waited anxiously for her return. At last I was called down to the recovery room and found a desperate situation. They had finished the operation, but despite maximal ventilation with oxygen, her skin was a greyish blue from lack of oxygen in the blood and she was close to death. A pall of hopelessness hung over the team. It was one of those situations where extreme measures feel paradoxically safe: there is nothing to lose. I asked the anaesthetist if I could replace the breathing tube in the baby's wind-pipe, which was risky because it might disturb the stitches that had closed off the fistula, or I might not be able to get the tube in again. She agreed dispiritedly. I put action to words and within a minute or so, to my delight the baby became pink again. She was out of immediate danger. It's hard adequately to describe the satisfaction of saving someone's life like this. When we looked at her other tube afterwards, we found it had been clogged by blood clots during the operation. Hence very little oxygen had been getting through.

She was still not out of the woods and required intensive support for many days afterwards. As I cared for her, I became aware of her personality: very feminine and graceful, and a quiet, likeable way about her. Don't ask me how I could tell all this in a newborn baby. I don't know myself, but it was there without a doubt, and I could even think of her as a friend. It was a pleasure to look after her.

And now I look after other people, some of whom also have a hole between their oesophagus and trachea, but this time it's caused by cancer and no operation in the world will put it right; they will inevitably die. There's a lesson for me, here, in humility. We doctors can, like Icarus flying, do such extraordinary things, but we are in truth so limited as well, and if we try to fly too close to the sun, the Apollonian image of perfect health, our wings fall away and we plummet to the earth, to the humus which is the etymological derivation of humility as well as of humiliation.

Multiple cultures

Both my parents were immigrants, I was brought up in a minority religion, Roman Catholicism, and I have a minority name. So, despite having always lived in England and been educated here so that I look and sound English, I often have a sense of not quite belonging. At school I would meet other boys whose families had lived in the same village or town for many generations. I would wonder wistfully what it was like to be so rooted in one place, among a whole community of similarly stable neighbours. My parents started from scratch in a new country. And yet, I don't regret this. My own experience has bred in me an antipathy to xenophobia for which I'm grateful.

> I remember a story my father told of when he was in the Army Medical Corps that was part of the Allied Forces sweeping into Germany in 1945. As a doctor, he joined the soldiers liberating the German prison camps. He saw for himself the horrors so often shown in documentaries, people reduced to walking skeletons (not unlike some of the cancer patients I care for), and dying, as he so graphically put it, like flies. But he noticed a strange thing. Some of the inmates, even though they should have responded to food and medicines he provided, did not improve; in fact they grew inexorably weaker and died. In the extremity of their dehumanisation by their captors, of their being regarded as less even than animals, they had entered the last, primal defence against

suffering of all animals by giving up the will to live. Such can be the effect of man's inhumanity to man.

All the reponsibility was on her shoulders. She was twenty, pregnant with her first child and her Bangladeshi mother was dying of cancer in a hospice. Dressed in a traditional sari she would come in to visit regularly and also to translate for her mother who spoke very little English. Whenever I talked with her, she was polite and attentive, but had that understandable, protective reserve of someone from an ethnic minority. I remember, though, that one day something changed, and it took me a while to work out what it was. Then I realised. She had decided to trust us, the wall had been lowered. I was touched, and also felt honoured. This was an act of courage on her part, a revealing of herself. I hope that we responded sufficiently to the confidence she placed in us. When her mother died, true to her culture the daughter threw herself to the ground by the bed and gave voice to the wailing mourning she had been taught. In a small way, I thought later, Islamic and Western traditions had touched. Perhaps, then, this is a good model for cultural and religious rapprochement: one step at a time and down among the grass roots, green with the sap of life.

Anima Mundi

Many years ago, I joined a group of hospice workers who would go regularly to a Russian Orthodox church nearby to talk with the priest who lived there. He was a small man, but his presence was very powerful and his gaze very direct. We had to go through the church to reach his room. There was always the evocative smell of incense, wood and stone, and icons of all sizes adorned the walls. Unlike Western churches there were hardly any chairs, but the screen separating the altar from the main body of the church was covered with gleaming, golden icons of saints and scenes from the Bible. During services, the chanting, which sounded to me like how I imagined the wind blowing across the endless Russian plains, rose and fell, a lament on behalf of the exiles who formed the congregation.

In the priest's room we would perhaps listen to a reading and then sit in silent meditation. After a while he would begin to speak, always with concentration, sincerity and commitment. He seemed to be listening deeply to something in the silence, some source that guided his words.

I remember one story he told concerning the overlap of religions. He visited a colleague who held no truck with anything apart from Christianity. The priest had with him a number of quotations and he asked his colleague if he could help him trace the source of these quotations in the Bible. Within a few minutes, the colleague had confidently assigned each extract to different books in the Bible. What he didn't know, however, was that they in fact came from the Baghavad Gita, one of the main sacred texts in Hinduism.

I was amused by this trickster approach and, too, found it heartening to think that passages from the writings of two very different religions could converge to that extent.

In my hospice, services of remembrance are arranged for relatives of those who have died. The main one is interdenominational. Often, many people attend and it is an emotionally charged occasion. At the beginning of the service, they write down the name of the deceased on a slip of paper and, in a very powerful part of the service, these names are called out, one by one. Later, the family, if they so wish, walk up to the front of the church, light a candle as a memorial, and place it in a container of sand along with a community of others, one giving light to the other; a deceptively simple religious act, real and hence strong, which we can all relate to and which effortlessly vaults religious walls.

Endgame

I've picked out a few memories for this chapter like pebbles from a beach. There are countless more, gleaming from the wash of the waves over them. I must continue my explorations, my re-membering of them. Will I find my lodestone? Perhaps they are all lodestones?

> I think continually of those who were truly great.
> Who, from the womb, remembered the soul's history
> Through corridors of light where the hours are suns,
> Endless and singing. Whose lovely ambition
> Was that their lips, still touched with fire,
> Should tell of the spirit clothed from head to foot in song.

And who hoarded from the spring branches
The desires falling across their bodies like blossoms...

Near the snow, near the sun, in the highest fields
See how these names are fêted by the waving grass,
And by the streamers of white cloud,
And whispers of wind in the listening sky.
The names of those who in their lives fought for life,
Who wore at their hearts the fire's centre.
Born of the sun, they travelled a short while towards the sun,
And left the vivid air signed with their honour.
(Spender 1960, p.621)

References

Bridges, R. (1960) 'Nightingales.' In L. Untermeyer (ed) *Collins Albatross Book of Verse*. London: Collins.

Craig, W. J. (ed) (1905) Hamlet. ll.ii. lines 323–327. In *Shakespeare Complete Works*. London: Oxford University Press.

Finlay, I. G. (1990) 'Sources of stress in medical directors and matrons.' *Palliative Medicine 4*, 5–9.

Herbert, G. (1966) 'Love (111).' In *The Nation's Favourite Poems*. London: BBC Books.

Heyse-Moore, L. H. (1996) 'On spiritual pain in the dying.' *Mortality 1*, 297–315.

James, W. (1977) *The Varieties of Religious Experience*. Glasgow: Fount.

Jones, A. (ed) (1966) *The Jerusalem Bible*. London: Darton, Longman and Todd.

Jung, C. (1964) *Man and his Symbols*. Garden City: Doubleday.

Reeves, P. (1999) *Women's Intuition*. Berkeley, California: Conari Press.

Rilke, R. M. (1975) 'Live the questions now.' In J.J.L. Mood (trans.) *Love and Other Difficulties*. London: Norton.

Spender, S. (1960) 'I think continually of those.' In L. Untermeyer (ed) *Collins Albatross Book of Verse*. London: Collins.

Whitman, W. (1960a) 'Song of myself.' In L. Untermeyer (ed) *Collins Albatross Book of Verse*. London: Collins.

Whitman, W. (1960b) 'When I heard the learn'd astronomer.' In L. Untermeyer (ed) *Collins Albatross Book of Verse*. London: Collins.

3

Early Challenges in Palliative Care from a Social Work Perspective

The Gift of Serendipity

Julia Franklin

Introduction

I have always loved the word 'serendipity'. I like the way it slides off the tongue. My dictionary says it is 'the faculty of making fortunate discoveries by accident' (Collins 1979). The word was apparently coined by Horace Walpole from a Persian fairytale 'The Three Princes from Serendip', in which the heroes possess this gift. I like serendipity being identified as a 'gift' because it gives the course of my professional life and what I might have brought to it a positive connotation, rather than the way I sometimes think of it; a series of happy accidents, being in the right place at the right time, one thing leading to another, although it is all of those things. Having the gift of serendipity, possessing the 'faculty of making fortunate discoveries by accident', is how it all started, and in some ways this is how it still proceeds.

I include in this chapter a description of what was happening in palliative care in 1982 when I became a member of the Bloomsbury Support Team attached to University College Hospital but working in the community of the London Borough of Camden. I mention what influenced me at the time, what kept me and indeed still keeps me in this type of work, and what personal strategies for survival I have developed.

The chapter includes what I have learned from working with people who are dying and bereaved, other colleagues who were influential at the time and how it has affected the way I work. I include factual information, some reflective discussion about motivation, personal development, and strategies I used for my own survival, leaving questions and thoughts which I hope will provoke further discussion for the reader.

My journey begins

I came into palliative social work as a 'late developer'. I had married young, had four children and was a full-time mother for 16 years. Then my husband was made redundant, so in my late thirties paid employment became a necessity. I became a part-time social work assistant in a local hospital. My qualifications were eight O levels, an unfinished diploma in Sociology, an offer of a place at London University to study part-time for the social work diploma which I hadn't been able to take up because of my husband's new job commitments, and 'university of life' experience to bring to my work.

From the hospital in which I worked, I was fortunate to be offered a secondment to study full-time for my diploma in social work, which I obtained in 1979. My subsequent experience after returning to work as a qualified social worker at the hospital on the surgical oncology unit made me see a huge gap in services for people who were undergoing treatment for advanced cancer. Two clients in particular, one, a young woman with children and the other, an elderly lady who wanted to remain at home to die, influenced my decision to want to work in palliative care, and in the community.

Another event influenced my decision to apply for the post of social worker to start up a 'new' palliative care community team. This event was a summer school in 1980 organised by the British Association of Social Workers. The subject was loss: loss in its widest sense and its effects both for people living in the UK and other cultures; loss as a result of unemployment, redundancy, old age, being a refugee, disability and long-term illness. The summer school looked at the changing roles of men and women, the loss of the 'normal child' for parents bringing up children and young people with a learning disability, including also the losses following bereavement.

The late 1970s and 1980s were times of enthusiasm in social work and medicine and other professions, too. New treatments for cancer were being researched. The hospice movement was spreading into the community. In the London Borough of Camden there were many resources being funded for people whose quality of life was impaired. The women's liberation movement and feminist ideas were becoming influential at this time. The Women's Therapy Centre in Hampstead was set up by Susie Orbach, the author of *Fat is a Feminist Issue* (Orbach 1978), and Luise Eichenbaum. There was a new Social Security Act being passed through parliament, which became the way to influence the social security system for people who were terminally ill, enabling them to obtain the appropriate benefits, and to remain at home, if that was their wish.

I was influenced by all these events, and others, as I started my career in palliative care. I realised that loss, change, death and bereavement are part of life and I had the experience of these issues suddenly making sense to me. With the benefit of hindsight, I can see how it all acted as a wonderful springboard for me and influenced the way I began to work in palliative care. The effects of a slowly dawning understanding of the theory of loss and change and how it had affected me and my wider family of origin, both in the present and in the past, informed my practice of working with families where someone was terminally ill. My mother had died when I was only 35 and now, seven years later, I became aware of my own mortality at an age and stage of my life when my older children were leaving home.

New challenges presented themselves. Advocacy and enthusiasm was required, and having a sense of drama and of humour helped. Perhaps I should explain what I mean about a sense of drama. The stage being set for a death scene, romantic notions of heroes and heroines, people looking at us, if we mentioned we worked with people who were dying as if we had halos around our heads; all these ideas spring into my mind as I reflect on what influenced me to have this type of career. Was I trying to be an angel of mercy? Did I think that by working so hard to enable 'death' to be handled in a more sensitive way, that I might avoid death myself?

I certainly feel, for myself, that the part of me that identifies with the characters in theatre, the plays, the dramas, the tragedies, the comedies, the laughter and the tears, enables me to empathise with people's emotional and physical pain in a way which then engages the more practical, manipulator-of-systems part of me, to be a change agent in the scheme of things.

Charismatic people

Palliative care, perhaps especially in those heady early days, involved people who were almost 'larger than life'. I particularly remember Susan Le Poidevin, who worked at St Christopher's Hospice in Sydenham for a while.

I attended one of her workshops on 'Breaking Bad News' early in my career. I liked her creative techniques in teaching about loss and grief. Her presentations could be outrageous and challenging but her enthusiasm was infectious and created heated discussion amongst her audience. The consequence, for me, was that I remembered the essence of the message; how important is the process of listening to the patient, and going at their pace, when sensitive issues are being addressed. She illustrated the variety of individual reactions to loss and grief by encouraging us to watch films, popular at the time, where the storyline, for example of parents separating and the effects on them as individuals and on the child involved, were pivotal to the plot. She taught me the importance, in teaching, especially when we need to engage both head and heart, of using techniques that challenge and touch us emotionally and where we can use our own experience of loss and grief to understand the theory. Sadly, Susan died from cancer in her early thirties, leaving behind a husband and very young child.

Professional associations

In 1982, when a meeting was held at St Christopher's Hospice to form a support group for social workers in palliative care, the scene was well and truly set for a career in working with people with a terminal illness and their carers, both before and after death. We often worked in isolation as social workers. We worked with, but were outnumbered by, nursing and medical colleagues. We were in the process of identifying our role, and how best we could be used within multi-disciplinary teams. The settings in which we were being asked to work were diverse, some NHS-funded, some independent and voluntary-funded, some had been established for years like St Joseph's Hospice in Hackney, and others were being set up in the first flush of enthusiasm. By forming one of the first professional associations in palliative care, we offered ourselves mutual support. We learned together and gained confidence in promoting the role we could perform in working within a model of holistic care, the central philosophy of the hospice movement.

There were only 25 social workers meeting at St Christopher's in 1982. In the last few years of the twentieth century there were over 200 members of what is now called the Association of Social Workers in Hospice and Specialist Palliative Care.

Bloomsbury

The Bloomsbury Support Team, as we were called in 1982, was formed to act as a link between a large teaching hospital and the community. The team offered advice on pain and symptom control and gave emotional, social and psychological support to people who were suffering from terminal cancer and to their carers, before and after death.

We had to find skills of tact and diplomacy in the way we introduced ourselves to ward sisters, medical and surgical staff within the hospital and to general practitioners and district nurses in the community. Death and dying were taboo subjects then and we needed to support one another in pioneering new ways of working. There was considerable resistance to a more open attitude to death and what could be seen as criticism of the way death and dying had been handled in the past.

My new colleagues were a part-time doctor and two, what would now be called, clinical nurse specialists. We were given an office, a table, and three chairs. We had only one telephone. I had the support of the social work team at University College Hospital. The nurses had a nurse manager in the community. There was a consultant radiotherapist who was 'responsible' for us all. On a day-to-day basis, however, we managed ourselves.

I am giving this detail to put into context what we all needed to bring to the pioneering situation in which we found ourselves. We needed to build up trust between ourselves, to support one another, to develop policies and procedures, forms, case notes and professional skills. We did not have a designated leader, but we all needed one another for support and discussion. We learned from one another and shared our successes and failures, and together became more confident in our role. That it did not end in 'failure' was a credit to us all, and maybe to the gift of serendipity.

Personal motivation

What sustained me during this period was the knowledge that with my nursing and medical colleagues, I could use my natural enthusiasm, passion and compassion and was able to channel anger and energy into campaigning for a better service for people whose life was limited. I really believed we had the opportunity to enable people to live a life 'as good as possible'. Serendipity had its part to play, in those early days. I made the 'fortunate discovery' by accident or circumstance that I had found a career to which I thought I had a contribution to make.

Support

One of the recurring concerns I have about working in palliative care over a period of years, is what we do with our feelings about seeing so many deaths, and sometimes, sad, unfair situations? How do we keep our batteries charged and avoid becoming burnt out?

I feel sure, for myself, that I was able to channel the anger I described above (from whichever source it emanated) into the campaign that I and others led to get the qualifying rules for Attendance Allowance and Disability Living Allowance waived for people who were terminally ill. As a team, we were seeing many people who were dying, but living in impoverished circumstances, who could not qualify for disability benefits, because they had to be suffering for six months before they could claim. Many people died before the benefit came through, causing great distress for their carers. Also their quality of life was diminished by not having sufficient finances. We thought this was an injustice. After all, they would not be claiming their retirement pension! So a challenge presented itself and fuelled by a sense of injustice and anger, after considerable effort both locally and nationally, we achieved our aims. It took from 1986 to 1990, but we got there! In fighting this campaign we found ourselves on TV in one of the first editions of *Watchdog*. We were in the 'corridors of power' in Westminster on several occasions, even at No. 10 Downing Street.

Later developments

The hospice movement was expanding and going out into the community. Organisations such as Help the Hospices and the National Hospice Council were becoming active and other professional associations for doctors, occupational therapists, physiotherapists, hospice managers and volunteers were being developed. Towards the end of the 1980s the AIDS epidemic was creating a need for specialised palliative care, and people with motor neurone disease were being accepted under the umbrella of palliative care. The voice of the hospice movement was being heard, awareness of the needs of people with terminal illnesses was being raised, and the effects of bereavement on adults and children were being acknowledged.

In relating these historical facts, I am demonstrating that, for me, working in palliative care continued to offer me new avenues to explore, opportunities to develop skills I did not know I had, and to serve on committees where I had the chance to contribute to informed discussion about future directions of palliative care. I had access to some excellent training, family therapy and experiential courses which enabled me to look at and acknowledge my own mortality. These were sustaining factors, keeping me stimulated and energised.

I had left school at 16. I had been offered the carrot of becoming a nurse or a teacher if I stayed on at school, but I could not see the point. Neither of these careers enthused me then, but in my forties and fifties I found my job required me to educate others and I discovered I actually knew enough to pass information on! Learning the necessary skills to engage and educate in the areas of grief and bereavement and working with bereaved children was very exciting. Somehow the capacity I found I had to absorb other people's sadness and pain, but not to allow it to overwhelm me, to know it was theirs and not mine was balanced by the positive feeling of sharing knowledge and skills that would help others. This was, and still is, a sustaining factor and a way of enabling me to cope in this type of work.

Conferences

In what other social work post would I have had the chance to travel and to go to international conferences? Obtaining funding to go to the first International Conference on Grief and Bereavement in Jerusalem in 1985 was a tremendous experience. Here, I learned about bibliotherapy – the use of literature to enable people to access and process feelings. On my return to the UK, I was able to incorporate it into my professional practice and to show others how to use it.

This conference had a lasting effect on me for a wide variety of reasons and stimulated me to apply for a Help the Hospices Fellowship in 1988, to go back to Israel to look at bereavement after-care in the hospice movement there. Travelling alone this time, spending three weeks out there, gave me the opportunity to meet so many interesting people and to gain confidence in addressing large audiences.

I learned much about the history of Israel and its problems at close quarters. I was made welcome by many people both secular and religious. I absorbed history and saw much beautiful countryside, as well as learning and being able to advise about the struggles people were having in setting up palliative care services.

I also had the opportunity to take part in conferences in Florence and Hamburg and to contribute to multi-disciplinary team teaching, which was very exciting. These experiences helped maintain the balance between being a practitioner and being an educator. Such a balance was necessary to protect me from the pain of patients and families, and therefore enabled me to 'recharge my batteries'.

What sustained and energised me over the years were these opportunities of sharing with others what can be achieved in relieving the suffering of people who are dying, and their carers. Being able to encourage others, helping them to see they had the skills, too, and to believe that from 'little acorns, oak trees grow' was a wonderful experience.

Learning from the dying

One of the things I have learned from working with people who have a limited life expectancy is not to put off too many plans in case I am defeated by death! In 1987, as part of our 'life's plan', we moved house to Chichester, along with my elderly father, who was nearing the end of his life. We had always planned to 'retire' down here and this move would give us time to put down our roots.

This change involved commuting to London for two years, until I found another job in the West Sussex area. The job I was successful in obtaining was to set up a new social work service in a hospice that had been open for 16 years and had never employed a social worker before. So, another challenge – how to use my London experience to help me do what needed to be done, in a very different setting, in a different part of the country. I knew I would need to be confident of my own professional identity; I would need to educate, inform and communicate with many people to convince them of the ideas I had to introduce in a social work department. The hospice was appointing clinical nurse specialists and developing a day hospice, so the setting was already going through a process of change. I knew it would not be easy for me.

I needed to think about support systems to sustain me, whilst I struggled to get social work accepted in this different culture. Personal supervision was important as was the Association of Hospice Social Workers in Specialist Palliative Care for its peer and local regional support groups.

I needed to have my leadership skills affirmed and to feel empowered amongst my own profession. A survival strategy for me at that time was my Professional Association and my participation in it. My three years of being Chair of the Association brought me almost up to my retirement; an exciting time when I could feel empowered again and able to share expertise with people coming into social work in palliative care for the first time. This was very important for me personally, at a time when I had left the close-knit team in London to start building links in a different setting in a different part of the country.

I mentioned briefly personal supervision, which is currently being given more value, especially by the nursing profession. Clinical supervision or personal support, whatever the title given, can be a sustaining influence. The concept has been incorporated into social work and counselling as a time to reflect on one's practice, look at the impact on ourselves of our work, review casework, consider future training needs and work out our personal and professional boundaries.

Final thoughts

During this reflection upon my personal experiences of working in palliative care, I have considered why I embarked on my own particular journey, what influenced me, how it affected me, what I needed to sustain me, what strategies for survival I developed and what I might have brought to the work.

What was the attraction for me of this experience and what did I think I had to offer? There was an excitement in pioneering new ways of working; a real sense of using one's whole personality as well as one's professional expertise. There was the impact and inspiration of meeting so many people with terminal cancer, from all walks of life, who were having to accept that their lives were limited. There was also a sense of being able to make a difference to this limited life span, whether it was through controlling pain and symptoms, offering advice about DSS benefits, obtaining grants from Macmillan Cancer Relief; or enabling people to put their affairs in order, emotionally or practically, according to their wishes.

What brought me and other social work, medical and nursing colleagues into this work, I believe, was a complex mix of personal qualities, leadership skills, altruism, advocacy, previous personal experiences of the death of a relative or friend superimposed on our own individual professional training.

I have mentioned the support and inspiration of colleagues, too numerous to mention by name, but always remembered by me. They were always there to laugh, cry, discuss ideas with me and to offer guidance and advice, which I hope I reciprocated.

Becoming aware of my own mortality has certainly sharpened my desire to live life to the full, and not to put off till tomorrow things I could do today, metaphorically speaking. When I retired from full-time paid employment in 1996, I went around the world for six months, visiting friends and family and experiencing other countries and cultures; something which I had always wanted to do. I was motivated by the knowledge that death might defeat me if I did not do it then! I know that my experience in palliative care, where so many people planned for futures which became impossible for them to achieve, influenced me in the timing of this decision.

This leads me to mention one final way of coping when working in palliative care; the importance of maintaining 'another life', the one we have 'after work'. For myself, my life was (and still is) enriched by being a parent and grandparent; by the support and care shown by friends and family; by my love of theatre, music and laughter. We each of us have 'another life' which needs to be lived, so that we maintain some sort of balance and perspective in our working life. Both parts of our lives then enrich and inform each other. Death becomes part of life, not the whole.

So how to draw all these threads together to make a 'good ending'? The phrase 'a good ending' is the very epitome of what we are trying to achieve in palliative care, and yet it has a double edge to it. For the bereaved the ending brings pain which is not as easy to control as the pain their loved ones suffered. It takes a long time to adjust to the process of loss and change, to reach the stage where the sorrow has a different quality, more like a 'tender longing than a hole in the heart' (Zunin and Zunin 1978, ch.2).

Writing this chapter for a book with the title *Journeys into Palliative Care: Roots and Reflections* has given me an opportunity to reflect on and re-experience my own personal journey. It has created in me many of the feelings familiar to bereaved people. It has given me the opportunity to remember the joys, the disappointments, the highs, the lows, the regrets and the achievements. I have been through my own process of remembering, re-experiencing and integrating some aspects of my career in palliative care. I am aware that the period 1982–1996 has already become part of the history of the hospice movement. It is a dynamic movement. It has to change and adapt and that will bring some pain and loss, but also transformation, integration and a future informed by its past.

I wonder if serendipity will have a part to play in that future?

References

Collins English Dictionary (1979). London: Collins.

Orbach, S. (1978) *Fat is a Feminist Issue.* London: Hamlyn.

Zunin, L. and Zunin, H. (1978) *The Art of Condolence.* London: Harper Collins.

4

On Becoming a Practitioner

The View of a Psychologist

Robin Trewartha

Introduction

My brief is to describe my history and how it appears to have shaped my professional development as a counselling psychologist. This is a personal statement explaining how I came to work in the helping professions. It describes a route forged out of many decisions and formative experiences with the promise of many twists and turns yet to come in this journey. In my early professional years in the probation and child protection fields (1968–1985), I worked with people experiencing major losses such as death, loss of liberty, innocence and family. In later years I spent time working with CRUSE Bereavement Care in the north-east of England and, later on, in Scotland (1985–1996). During my time in London (1997 – present), I have worked with people who were dying, with asylum seekers for whom loss is an ever-present feature, and in employment assistance and private practice. Today I have a special interest in critical incident management and assist organisations to anticipate avoidable risk, and deliver clinical services to groups and individuals after those risks turn into unavoidable incidents. This includes organising and delivering debriefing work and post-trauma counselling.

Beginnings

As my name betrays, I am a man with Cornish roots although I was born in Devon, shortly after the end of the Second World War. For 18 years I lived in a small village, close to the City of Exeter, but far enough away to be a separate community. I was the youngest of three, with an older brother and sister. I recall a distant and wary relationship with my father, now deceased, and ever-changing relationships with my mother who remarried and remains fit and lively to this day. My childhood life was not a haven; the domestic disharmony and eventual separation of my parents was a major formative experience. I developed a reputation as a pugilistic and often unco-operative child in my primary and early secondary years. My mother despaired of the number of NHS glasses that I went through, fighting over every real and imagined slight to my sense of right or wrong.

Despite the domestic tensions, my early life was privileged, not so much in material terms, but because the environment in which I was reared was relatively predictable, stable and comfortable. My 'playground' covered square miles and the local children roamed freely in the woods and fields in a way that seems unheard of today. The village had its own primary school located just a few yards away from the fourth, and final, home my family occupied in the village. This home was the site of a family business, a small general store, tea-room and guest house.

In 1958, at the age of 11 years, I made the large move beyond my home and that village. I continued to lead a relatively privileged life in the sense that I won a scholarship to the local direct grant school in Exeter where I spent my years up to A levels. Secondary schooling detached me from my peer group in the village and accelerated a growing sense of myself as an 'outsider'.

I determined my future career early on, in my mid-teens. My initial aspiration was to join the technical services of the BBC. This was fanned by the frequent visits by BBC personnel to our guest-house. The large and mysterious transmission vans held a fascination for me, but my early ambition was thwarted; after O levels, it was clear that I was never going to succeed in the engineering sciences. Around that time, I read a book about the work of a probation officer and recall a strong sense of identity with the young anti-hero who sailed close to the wind. This caught my imagination and I determined to head for the probation service. I think I decided that if I was to end up in court then I'd better be sure I was on the right side of it!

My adult years

I took the first step towards my goal in 1965 when, aged 18 years, I left my family home to go to university, returning only two or three times in the vacations. I was married immediately after graduating in Psychology and Social Administration in 1968. Today it seems strange to be married at 21 years and, indeed, a parent at 22 but it all seemed so normal at that time. The so-called liberated 1960s saw many in my generation take family responsibilities at an early age although the accompanying sense of my own certainty and confidence was to evaporate around a dozen years later.

I made it into the probation service, just three months over the minimum age of 21 years, one of a small growing band of graduate entrants. Someone so precocious, ambitious and seemingly clear-sighted needed the apprenticeship provided by that demanding service. These were sobering years and, from many clients, old and young, I learned the basic facts of life about surviving on minimal incomes, in inadequate housing and often in emotionally draining, if not destructive environments.

I celebrated 15 years of marriage and had the gift of two children whom I continue to enjoy many years on. Sadly, I did not stay married and I left the family home in 1983. During several difficult years in the 1980s I was unable to sustain close relationships, and I came close to despair at one stage. I will say more about this later.

I moved to Scotland to take up a university teaching post in 1985 and, in 1989, I resolved to start up my own business as a trainer and educator. I had always sworn, from my earliest days, that I would not go into a family business again as I knew something of the price paid for so doing. I had to change some fundamental thinking to take on such a risky venture, but I was helped when I realised that this would not be *family* business. No-one else need lose out from the venture. So I continued with the plan, helped by a financial cushion willed to me by a much loved aunt who died in 1987. Starting the consultancy resurrected for me the notion of service, born many years before when I worked in the family business.

I also revived an appreciation of direct work with clients and over the next ten years I was involved in many ventures that broadened my horizons and work experience. I formulated a commitment to take professional training as a chartered counselling psychologist, building on my earlier undergraduate and post-graduate education in psychology and education. It seems to me no real surprise that I should commit to a new career in counselling in those later years. It may be no coincidence either that I was privileged in a different way when I entered a second, successful marriage that has continued now for nearly ten years.

How my biography informs my practice

From this account, I can discern a number of professional issues which I conceive here as a series of meetings with my shadow side.

Meeting myself

It has taken me quite some time to experience individuation or, as Guggenbuhl-Craig describes it, a 'flowering of the basic design of an individual human existence, the experience of individual meaningfulness' (Guggenbuhl-Craig, 1982, p.128). I suspect I was helped and hindered, probably in about equal measure, by the books and the training I undertook over the years. The ideas of Transactional Analysis (TA) theory came to me as a breath of fresh air in the 1970s. In particular, the concept of Drivers made immediate sense to me. Five Drivers are identified in the TA literature as Be Perfect, Hurry Up, Be Strong, Try Hard and Please (Kahler 1978). The word 'Driver' is used because a person has a compulsion to follow powerful messages repeated many times in early life. Running with that compulsion helps maintain the individual's sense of contentment (or OKness). Although each of us can demonstrate all five Drivers, it is usual for one to be in the forefront. In my case, the 'Hurry Up' Driver seemed to fit me well. This message – received from adult caretakers – was absorbed in an environment where there was a lot to do and pressure to get it done quickly. The message to work hard was, literally, chalked up on the wall and my mother demonstrated to me how to get a result.

In practical terms, the 'Hurry Up' Driver motivated me not to be long attending to tasks. Attending takes time and 'Hurry Up' prompted me to think that there was too little time to do all that there was to do (rather in the style of the White Rabbit in *Alice in Wonderland*). In particular, 'Hurry

Up' ensured I got out of the door to play sooner, rather than later. In the longer term, the same message provided a justification for not taking time to be sensitive to feelings, to processing them and reflecting on what to do with them. It is not a large leap of reasoning to see how this Driver might undermine my emotional health.

In time, I learned that 'Hurry Up' was closely connected to the sense I had of being the 'outsider'. Why? In English, the terms 'be long' and 'belong' have little discernable difference in sound but large differences in meaning. Given that these messages are often absorbed when language skills are just developing, it should come as no surprise that 'Hurry Up' became confused in my mind with not belonging as well. I discovered later that the experience of being an 'outsider' is common to many clients and often associated with the 'Hurry Up' Driver.

I recall one client whose partner suffered a violent death. He buried himself in his work to try and forget. The pain of imagining what she may have suffered seemed too much to bear and he wanted it over. Avoidance was an understandable strategy for him to use. Working through an important anniversary and a court case were both distressing events. However, he learned to use therapy as a safe place in which to *take time* for those feelings to be expressed. I believe the client benefited from my gentle encouragement and challenges.

Similar situations arose in my work with asylum seekers and people sent to penal institutions where carefully measured engagement was essential with people who had experienced a lot of oppression or were capable of offering it to others. Thus, in one Prison Unit, where 'Don't Belong' was built into the social and physical fabric, I met a prisoner used to fighting, violence and segregation. These were key strategies for protecting his own safety and privacy. In a slow and gentle process of confrontation, I used my own example to demonstrate a different way of being. It is quite unsettling when a male, such as myself, with all the sound and appearance of a 'macho' guy, breaks the social rules! I think I helped him see through my first appearance. Perhaps he learned that there was more to life than appearances and more than one route to the specific goal of obtaining liberty.

A second element of my own upbringing that I have had to face emerges from my understanding of attachment theories and, more particularly, adult attachment research. The idea that childhood attachment styles mature in adulthood is relatively straightforward, but what form they take, and how they express themselves is not so obvious. Bartholomew and Shaver (Simpson and Rholes 1998, Chapter 2) asserted that attachment styles were manifestations of 'internal working models' of childhood extended into adulthood. Bartholomew laid emphasis on the quality of early attachment relationships in laying the foundation of a sense of self and an *orientation to others*.

Bartholomew created four outlooks or adult attachment styles, each one similar to TA thinking about 'OKness':

- Secure (positive of self and other), or I'm OK, you are OK.

- Pre-occupied (negative of self and positive of other), or I'm not OK, you are OK.

- Fearful (negative of self and other), or I'm not OK, you are not OK.

- Dismissing (positive of self and negative of other) or I'm OK, you are not OK.

At a superficial level, I demonstrated a secure attachment style but, in truth, my responses minimised intimacy, and were more consistent with the dismissing adult attachment style.

It took time for me to learn that I had failed to trust others during my formative years. I suspect this was obvious to some but I had to learn about it in my own way and in my own time. I had not learned how to take risks and provide *appropriate* protection for myself. In adulthood I did not respond differently to changing circumstances or to appreciate that I *could* respond differently. I hung on to archaic solutions that worked as a child for a while, but were of little value in adulthood. It was too easy to hide behind a superficial self-confidence. If that did not work, then a bit of aggression usually managed to make up the difference, as it did for my client in the Prison Unit.

What were the implications of all this for my own therapeutic practice? I came to understand how unresolved developmental needs in the personal history of client and therapist impacted on therapeutic outcomes. I learned to recognise the impact of my own upbringing on each therapeutic event and to accept that my professional expertise and skill, alone, would not lead to a successful therapeutic outcome. This may be self-evident to many trained therapists 'at home' with notions of transference, projection and the labyrinthine activities of the unconscious, but *knowing* is not the same as *acting on* the information. I knew the basics but it took me time to trust others and, more importantly, to trust my *own* experiences and intuitions. For too long I had allowed others to define them for me. I was, in the jargon, over-socialised. My values and judgements had been thoroughly and very carefully installed *and unquestioned.*

I really needed to appreciate this at a deeper emotional level but my reactive and dismissing style worked against that. It took me time to recognise this and to start exploring it and to 'allow' me into the equation. In doing so, I started to relate to my own shadow in a safe place and entered into therapy, initially in personal development groups, 'T' groups and, later, in individual work. During that journey I have had to meet my own anger and the anger of others.

I was helped by individual therapy in more recent years, learning that I do not have to be 'alright' to be loved or accepted. 'Alright' and 'all right' both apply here but became confused in my formative years. My pugilism, contrariness and argumentativeness reflected a stubbornness that once led me to argue that right is wrong and black is white. I had to be right all the time. Now I see it as a manifestation of insecurity, indeed, a response to threats to my sense of identity. It seems to me that I was only acceptable to myself on the basis of 'having' to be right. I could not feel alright, or OK, as Transactional Analysis would put it, without being 'all right' (Stewart and Joines 1987, 119ff). Acceptability to self and my sense of OKness were inextricably linked and, for that reason, I subscribe now to Guggenbuhl-Craig's (1982) view that, as a helper, I am often at my most dangerous when I convince myself *I am* right. To avoid this, it pays to be 'knocked off my perch' from time to time. Now I welcome those unsettling experiences, rather than resist them. Many clients have been excellent teachers.

For example, as a predominantly brief therapy practitioner, I have had to learn the limitations of the brief methodology. The only time I ever had a complaint made about my own clinical practice arose from a client with aspects of a narcissistic personality. Although I spotted some of these features, I still persuaded my supervisor to let me work with this client rather than assess and refer on. I believed there were communications exercises that could enable him to negotiate more effectively with others. In truth, it is more likely that he engaged my own narcissism in his challenge that 'no-one had been able to help him' before. I think, now, that the client expected no-one to help him and, indeed, worked hard to ensure that that happened. The two of us spent much time on our joint intention to test one another to failure or, indeed, to see who could fail the most splendidly!

On a more positive note, some of those seemingly less desirable qualities had their uses. I was well practised in avoidance behaviour and I knew what had and had not worked for me. Recently, I saw a traumatised client and recommended a visualisation exercise. I offered him a scenario that gave ample space for movement and choice of travelling companion. The client was very moved by the relationship he chose to visualise. For him the freedom of movement and choice was essential and he seemed to appreciate my sensitivity to his need. Providing maximum 'space' and a range of choices helped the client to address long-standing unfinished business with a now-departed family member. Insight into the strategies I had employed to avoid resolution of my own problems in my own past improved my ability to be a support to this client. At the same time, I did not assume *my* solutions would work well for him. Knowing we had a common experience gave me confidence to help this client find his own answers through his own actions.

Meeting despair

The period 1986–89 represented, without a doubt, the lowest point in my life to date. The one saving grace was the land around my home, which enabled me to get lost in my large garden and on long, rambling walks around the Sidlaws. Even so, I did not take kindly to living alone and a lack of commitment or direction in life took its toll. This was the one time in my life when I began to wonder whether it was all worthwhile. This ended in 1988 when I heard a local radio broadcast early one Sunday morning. A man had been found dead from exposure in Glen Tilt and all the indications were that it was a suicide. This item made me realise that I had a choice. I could go out of the world with 15 seconds of radio fame, or I could use the time left to me to make more of the opportunities available.

This experience taught me something about working with people in despair. It also made me more aware of the rather threadbare relationship I had had with my father that had proved a psychological handicap for many years. The handicap lay in a reduced ability to make and sustain commitments that others seemed to enter without question. I also came to recognise that I had minimised the emotional cost to myself on the two occasions I left home, although I knew the distress it would create for others. I *appeared* not to care, but the defences I used in making those moves impaired my ability to be intimate. It took me many years to face my self, my own actions and the feelings I had stored up. In particular, feeling guilty was an uncommon experience for me and it would seem that, for a long time, I worked hard to make it stay that way. There were no short cuts to facing up to those feelings of guilt, inadequacy and incompetence. I valued the fact that I was able to do this work at my own pace in group and individual therapy even though the learning, and the hurting, were prolonged.

Even so, like many people with disability, I learned to adapt. In time I gave myself the opportunity to learn about relating to my past and roots. In time, I worked *with* other guides and learned not be ashamed of my history. I was helped here by Harry Chapin, an American singer song-writer who told stories in his songs. I was able to learn new ways of relating from the heroes and heroines in his often lengthy tales. Many were updated versions of that tale of triumph over adversity that so much influenced me in my adolescence. Chapin was a bountiful source of 'Allowers' that helped me reframe the less helpful aspects of my Driver behaviour. So, 'Hurry Up' became an ability to fly by the seat of my pants. 'Be Strong' became a permission to provide a *temporary* rock for clients in crisis. This last was valuable to the many clients I met who were feeling disorientated, confused and distressed by trauma.

So, some of my less helpful behaviours were challenged, sometimes transformed, but often simply accepted. I developed confidence in my ability to make choices and to move in a different direction. Also, I recognised that clients can redirect their own energies and that I can contribute to the process by example. Thus, I do not use words alone to encourage a client with a 'Hurry Up' Driver to slow down. I will demonstrate it by a congruent tone and delivery.

For example, I recall one client who arrived in a state of despair. She mustered enough energy to come to see me, but she was not committed to her work and found even leisure reading uninteresting. She had not visited her family doctor and was reluctant to do so. In this first assessment session, we came around to the subject of things that interested her and the list was short. However, we talked about films. *Gaslight* had been screened recently. This prompted her to open up and talk rapidly as she recalled the storyline and spoke about her relationship with her partner. This had been strained by recent events and she was feeling manipulated by him and angry towards him. She felt misunderstood and unappreciated. She found it difficult to approach him with requests for support since she expected him to 'understand'.

I was able to respond by talking in a slower, measured delivery, making explicit some of my own misunderstandings of what she was saying and I lent forward with a furrowed brow, to ask what was wanted of me and, of him. Her subsequent focus on the lack of support led her to decide that she would contact her doctor and that she would ask for time away with her partner in the near future. She did not really need much from me other than to provide the space in which to clarify her sense of confusion and alienation. I doubt she was aware of the invitation to slow down and take time, but it may have been acted on. The client adjourned our follow-up session in order to go on a short break with her partner and, when we did meet again, she had accepted an NHS referral to see a local counsellor at her surgery and was sounding and looking more confident and motivated.

In this situation, I had done relatively little, but I believe talking about that story opened a door to her. Quite routinely, now, I will ask about favourite stories, story tellers and musicians and this has led me to appreciate the power of biblio-therapy.

Meeting others

In that shop during childhood, I learned to listen, understand and sometimes, to shut off the words and to 'listen' in a different way. This experience taught me that effective communication meant attending to several different channels. Of course, I did not regard what I did in those early years as anything special, but corner shops in the 1950s and 1960s did provide one place where customers could express themselves openly to someone outside their close family and church.

If this strange training school helped me in some ways, working in the business was exacting in others. I met people professionally in large numbers, as we three children did a lot of 'helping out', in the home and business – from weeding the garden to serving in the shop and tea-room. Another consequence of all this was that home was never a private place. Serving others required careful attention to boundary-making, which I did effectively, perhaps too effectively in that I built some solid, almost certainly impermeable emotional boundaries.

It took time to make those boundaries more malleable but I now regard myself as 'good' at boundary management. It was easier for me to loosen boundaries and explore safe limitations than it might have been to tighten chaotic ones. Today, I am fluid in my approach to my work. Indeed, in trauma management, servicing needs often depends on the ability to adapt quickly as circumstances are prone to change every day, even every hour or minute.

For example, on one occasion I was invited to join a critical incident team working abroad. As usual, the team was put together at very short notice. It requires a certain personality or flexibility of action to respond to such invitations. More importantly, once on site there is no rule book. Every situation is unique and, for clients, it has no parallel or precedent. It is not simply a question of organising debriefings, 'counselling' individuals or assessing needs in accordance with some pre arranged rules. Often there is a need to provide practical services and simply be 'available'. This includes being patient when no-one requires your services.

Service is an old-fashioned term but I think counsellors can still learn something from it. In my formative years I did not *think* about service, I did it. It was a practice that required me to be available to others seven days a week, sometimes for over twelve hours a day. It meant attending to another, intensely for short periods of time, without becoming so absorbed that a similar service could not be provided to the next customer. I am not proposing that the modern counsellor should work a twelve-hour day; the spirit of service is not concerned with the *quantity* of work completed. It is, however, concerned with the quality of relationships. This may require professionals to demonstrate the core

Rogerian conditions (Rogers 1961) but respect and regard can be shown in *actions* that might appear, at first sight, rather less than unconditional. For me, the value of 'service' includes actions that challenge the client to participate. Service may involve giving of ourselves to create a shared professional relationship, but it is also about the initiation of a number of responsible actions to enable it to get off the ground. This includes finding out what the client is willing and able to contribute to the process. For example, it can include giving and receiving loving confrontations. Respect for the other can be manifest in:

- establishing ground rules for our interventions; for example, in making concrete contracts with clients

- giving information when it is needed; how many counsellors are reluctant to say, in words or deeds, that 'there are things I know that you do not know'?

- asking permission to make interpretations; how many of us are so well trained that we forget we are using metaphors much of the time when we respond to clients

- being ever open to contradiction by one's client; how many of us are surprised when a client is assertive and how do we respond?

- using language that gives permission to expose and work on the power relationship that exists between client and counsellor.

Let me offer a practical example. Many clients have no prior knowledge of counselling and I think all clients need to make an informed choice about something as important as a therapeutic relationship. I suspect that few of us offer a free initial consultation to facilitate that process and foster choice, at that stage, by inviting a client to take time to meet other clinicians.

Privilege is another old-fashioned term I apply to professional relationships and one that therapists may dismiss even more readily than 'service'. Privilege implies not only some special position; it may imply a special position *over* the other. In this context, then, the term 'privilege' is uncomfortable but it *is* the case that I have expertise and clients consult me *because* of that fact. Withholding information means that I am not sharing knowledge that is available to me. In my view, that constitutes an unacceptable privilege. In practice I believe that the therapist can, and should, make explicit the nature of the privileged relationship. It is not only about making explicit the rules of confidentiality, although this is vital, but also about acknowledging differences. The counsellor and client are *not* equally responsible for making and maintaining a *professional* relationship. Ignoring difference will not make it go away, but it is a sin of omission that fosters abuse and disregard of the client. In child protection, I learned that the most effective abusers are good at creating cosy, collusive, 'shared' but secretive relationships.

To illustrate, I recall my work with a father whose son had died unexpectedly. The son had been seriously injured in a fall some two years before; the father was living and working in the UK and he had been separated from his family for many years. This client came to counselling because his family thought he needed it. The family and this client both expected him to be 'told' what was happening and what needed to be done. Further, he came to me in the immediate aftermath of the loss when 'counselling' may not have been the most appropriate intervention. As someone with no prior experience of counselling, this client did not know about ethical contract formation and it was my responsibility to introduce the subject even if the client was impatient to tell his story. This client did not start until the implications of some of these similarities and differences were aired. You could say I *did* 'start where the client was'; he wanted information and questions answered and talking about a contract seemed accepted as part and parcel of that. But I doubt that this containment would be viewed as 'person-centred'. The client wanted to get started and 'be told'. My information included guidance on the limitations of his preferred approach to counselling and I gave prior warning about the discomfort that would – and did – arise from not answering all of his questions!

Meeting trauma, loss and death

My maternal great grandmother lived with us for a number of years, ruling our family – the children, at least – in the tradition of the best Victorian matriarch. In my early teens, death came to us when this grand old lady died and her daughter, my grandmother, followed her not so long after. As it happened, on both occasions, I was away from home on camping holidays and no-one thought to call me home for the funerals. In keeping with the 1950s and 1960s, it seems that young people were kept away from death. I was protected from it, but doubt I am the better for it.

I was not faced with death in the family again until the untimely death of my father-in-law in the mid-1970s. This was followed by my own father's death in 1981, after a stroke and lengthy illness. Both experiences provided me with opportunities to re-evaluate my life. I developed a growing awareness that I did not need to follow in my father's footsteps. I stopped wishing my life away and became more aware of my current experiences. Not all were welcome but even those feelings of despair led me, in due time, to be less fearful of uncertainty. I learned to respond to loss and bereavement in an increasingly sensitive and authentic way, but only by the following very indirect route.

In my teens, I was told that a spur road was to be built off the 'new' M5. When it arrived, after I had left home, it was driven up the middle of the valley that joined my home village to the city. The road paved over a small river, overshadowed and made redundant an ancient Saxon bridge and destroyed the tranquillity of a rural community. I felt much anger over that road-building project, which seemed to me an act of vandalism. It was an act that left me with only memories of many childhood experiences. I have kept postcards of the way it used to be before those changes were made. Outrageous as it might seem, this building project raised more feelings in me than some of those earlier family deaths. This road tarmac'd my playground and obliterated the places where I had spent many happy hours. I felt this project disconnected me from my already fragile roots.

This experience helped me be empathic towards many others who responded to loss by avoidance and displacement. For instance, I have met many clients who have been 'blocked' by the experience of sudden death and trauma. It is not uncommon to feel guilty or to accept some fault for not responding 'properly'. I have known clients to 'blame' their current behaviour on an obviously traumatic event only to find even earlier unresolved losses are the 'real' cause of the problem. I, too, learned later how my outrage over the road project concealed unresolved issues relating to deaths in my own family and am now more aware of that redirection of energy in others.

For example, I was working with a man who had been involved in one of the devastating IRA attacks on London. I did not meet the client until some 20 years after the event. He was aware that his life, and career, had not moved in a positive direction. He had tried numerous sources of help and support but the traumatic incident seemed to exercise a powerful influence over him. The client did not 'blame' the specific incident but, in many ways, the fact that he did not made me more alert to post-traumatic stress. What did emerge, in time, was that the impact of that bombing eclipsed unresolved feelings about the death of his grandfather in his teenage years. As these remained unaddressed, the client's mental and physical well-being slowly deteriorated. Fortunately, Traumatic Incident Reduction (TIR) (Bisbey and Bisbey 1999, p.140) makes plain the possibility that traumas can be layered one upon another. My open-mindedness, informed by my training, served me well in this instance. The powerful impact of the bombing was so overwhelming that even the experienced practitioner might be distracted by such obvious events. In this particular instance, the client – like myself – had not been able to say his farewells to an important relative. It is quite likely that his childhood fantasies, such as feeling responsible for the event, may have moved with him into adulthood and undermined his ability to make and sustain close relationships. Again, my work was informed by my own unhappy experiences, but not blocked by them.

In other instances, my own experience has enabled me to understand that destruction can lead to a rebirth. On one memorable return visit to my childhood home, I visited the long-closed Tyne Valley railway line in a different part of the village. I found it neglected and reclaimed by the wild. My two children were able to share the fleeting pleasure of watching a roe deer feeding just before getting wind of our presence and rushing off. Here an unhappy change had an unexpected pleasurable spin-off. More recently, after a gap of many years, I returned to the village with my second wife to find how little some things had changed. I could swear the church door had not been painted in 40 years! It seems that the eye of this beholder is rather capricious; maybe context and relationship have something to do with it!

This idea that the same facts or situation can be viewed in different ways at different times is important in therapeutic work. One client came to me with panic attacks and, as a frequent flyer for her business, she was finding it more and more difficult to travel. This young woman had moved home, aged eight years, arriving at some anonymous, distant town. Her parents had done the 'right' things and taken her to see the new home before the move, but an older sister was not intending to make the move with her and this was not fully appreciated by the child. It seemed to me that the older sister represented a secure base to the child, my client, who responded to the loss by developing an increasingly dismissive adult attachment style. I sensed that insight into these relationships would not be enough; it might be dismissed as insubstantial. Instead, the client and I focused on this move as a first lesson in adaptation that now enabled her to earn her living as a traveller. The loss of her sister was turned into the gift from her sister who helped the client start to live independently. At the same time, the client was able to say 'thank you' to her sister for the age-appropriate supports she had provided in those early years. This reframe, and some more cognitive desensitisation strategies, appeared to remove the symptoms within a two-month period and, as far as I know, there has been no recurrence of the symptoms.

Presently I practise in the employment assistance sector where people often arrive in counselling saying, 'I never thought I'd be asking to see you, but ...' What I have learned from this is that few of us know how we will react to unusual events. Bank raids, sudden deaths, major incidents or redundancy have in common the destruction of what is accepted as 'normal'. They create uncertainty. By contrast, bereavement is a life event that is unavoidable but the near-certainty of meeting it does not make our specific experiences any easier to accommodate. Although personal experience of an incident may benefit a therapist, sharing it with clients may not help. The same event will not be perceived in the same way. My own experience can be a distraction and stop me *exploring* it from the client's point of view.

From clients and therapy I gained insight into the confusion and struggle promoted by crisis, trauma, loss or bereavement and the feelings of guilt, failure and despair that can be generated. This helped me to face fears of 'getting it wrong', or feeling responsible for things such as the death of loved ones or the separation of my parents. Also, I had to discern such events from the avoidable failures, the lost relationships and life opportunities, and to appreciate how each contributed to an existential sense of uselessness. With this insight, comes a kind of resilience that is valuable in trauma-related work. I am more helpful when I can absorb raw and primitive feelings and, at the same time, respond rapidly to major changes in mood and circumstances. To meet labile and unpredictable emotional events requires a well-grounded worker.

...and tomorrow?

It seems I have been many people over my 55 years. The career path that I have followed seems to reflect different stages in my own development; in the administration of justice at a time when I had a vision to pursue, in child protection when I was a parent of young children, and in education when I felt the need to pass on the benefits of my experiences and learning. Today, I have integrated these strands into a third career as counsellor – where education has its place, protection of the vulnerable is rather more sophisticated and where clients seem to make the most progress when our two visions make sense of one another.

Changes in my career reflected shifts in my life style and, doubtless, shifts in my personality. So if I am what I eat, I am certainly what I chose to do. I have had the good fortune to be given enough time to *grow* a fulfilling career and to learn that it did not need to follow a single path. I have transformed some of my personality limitations into professional strengths through my own therapy and personal development. In particular, on my arrival in London in 1997, I found a training programme and a profession where I am, at last, at home. It is one which I elected to join, rather than one others thought might be 'good' for me. So, today, my sense of not belonging has developed into a respect for privacy for self and others and an ability to empathise with clients who struggle not to belong, often out of fear of losing their own sense of identity. I have long since ceased to be surprised by the sychronicity which brought certain clients to my doorstep at certain times.

I may have been shaped by my history but I have a strong sense that my roots are in the future. Roots provide nourishment for growth and, for someone with few conventional roots, it seems more helpful to look to tomorrow for my home. I am aware of tasks unaddressed. For instance, I have yet to learn to forgive with any grace and fluency. I hold on to resentment, not quite so strongly, but just enough to keep me looking behind, not ahead, at times of insecurity. Maybe the loss of that playground, or the loss of certainty that accompanied the death of President John Kennedy and the loss of respect for aspects of authority (particularly following the disgrace of Nixon) continue to foster disbelief and a lack of trust. I am not helped here by any social pressure to forgive for, sadly, the last person I seem able to forgive is myself. In my more reflective moments, I am aware that these social and spiritual imbalances will require my attention in due time.

References

Bisbey, L. and Bisbey, S. (1999) *Brief Therapy for Post-Traumatic Stress Response.* Chichester: Wiley.

Guggenbuhl-Craig, A. (1982) *Power in the Helping Professions* Texas: Spring Books.

Kahler, T. (1978) *Transactional Analysis Revisited.* Little Rock: Human Development Publications.

Rogers, C. (1961) *On Becoming a Person: A Therapist's View of Psychotherapy.* London: Constable.

Simpson, J. A. and Rholes, W. S. (1998) *Attachment Theory and Close Relationships.* New York: Guilford Press.

Stewart, I. and Joines, V. (1987) *TA Today.* Nottingham: Lifespace Publishing.

5

Explorations in Creative Writing
'I Recharge Myself from My Experience'

Gillie Bolton

Are you sitting comfortably? Then I'll begin.

> *Listen with Mother* BBC Radio Home Service.

Grief only grows on a branch strong enough to bear it.

> Victor Hugo, song set to music by Benjamin Britten

A story: The patient who gave me a job

The nights were all the same, a pattern of anxiety-provoking unpredictable tasks. A teaching hospital in 1980. I still hate the smell.

Rick was a young man with a girlfriend, reggae music tapes and leukaemia. Lots of friends of all shapes and sizes visited and gave their blood, or part of it.

In the day, professors, consultants, sister, registrars, and me, all talking about what to do with him and his blood, his chest, his mouth infection. In the night, every six hours for five months, I gave him injections, took blood off, put up drips.

He got better, went home and I saw him on the street after I had left the hospital. He looked okay, not pleased to see me. All those stabs, jabs and 'one more times'.

Then in the evening paper at home, I read that he had jumped off the top of a tower block of flats. Dead.

Did we tell him what I realised along the way? All those things, procedures, drugs would only make him well for a short while. It always comes back and kills you in the end. He seemed to know but in all those dark hours we never talked properly.

There was a registrar who worked with me then. He probably made more real contact with our patients than any of us. He was a jolly, wide-faced young man who never turned up to parties, hated his father and said if he got leukaemia all he wanted was a desert island and twenty bags of blood. He killed himself when he became a consultant.

Ten years later, at the Hospice, Rick's girlfriend was in a bed, dying with the same kind of leukaemia that Rick had. So pleased to see me. We talked about Rick and dying young and couldn't find reasons. Squaring a very sad circle. (Bill Noble 2002)

Bill had had that squared circle of story hanging around in his head for all those years; he says it still makes him shudder. Writing it has not taken it out of his head, has not prevented him from working on it. But it has deepened and expanded his memory, and what it means to him: the story now has elements which he hadn't thought about before. He has no wish to write the definitive account of these events, because that would prevent him from continuing to work upon it, prevent it from continuing to grow. He said: 'This writing is not an emptying of me onto the paper, as I feared before I started, but an enriching.' In ten years there will be another version which will represent his thinking then. This is deep and effective reflection upon practice.

This chapter is about how reliving vital life experiences, thoughts and feelings through writing, and then sharing them with others can make a big difference for practitioners, patients and relatives. Writing and talking about such horrors as these of Bill's do not make them go away, but they certainly channel the energy in a much more positive way, as well as encouraging support and advice from colleagues. Bill Noble is a palliative physician. The theme the group were writing about on this occasion was simply *an important event.*

Having a conversation with oneself, which is what the experience of this kind of writing can be like, can help clarify issues and increase self-understanding. My sister said to me recently: 'But you know who you are!' Well, I think I certainly don't know who I am, in an existential sense. Though owning a passport does help with some sort of certainty that I do at least exist. But she didn't really mean that. She meant: 'You have something you know is worth doing in the world.' And of course she's right. I didn't always, but I have for the last 15 years or so. We all deserve to have some sort of an understanding, not perhaps of who we are, but something coherent about our life and what we do. I am going to tell you a story about something which I think is worth my spending some of my best energies saying, and doing with people. I am also going to tell you a story, actually several interwoven stories, from the carers of terminally sick people, and their own quest for finding out more about themselves.

Listening to a story

There are two parties involved in story-telling. There is the story-teller, me in this particular case. This chapter is the story I am telling you today, one to which I am certain you will pay attention. You are the other party, my listener and interlocutor. This certainty that you will listen attentively, and respond imaginatively and from depths of yourself to what I have to say, is perhaps what my sister was talking about.

Some of you will remember hearing the words with which I began this chapter (the opening to *Listen with Mother* on the BBC Radio Home Service), as well as the Brahms lullaby that was the programme's theme tune. Some also will recall what my husband showed me the other day, saying: 'Do you remember this?' – as if I could forget the test card which sat on the BBC television screen before *Children's Hour* came on. It seemed to remain there endlessly until Andy Pandy, Bill and Ben the Flower Pot Men, or Muffin the Mule appeared. We certainly had our attentions engaged thoroughly by then.

Every one of us needs and deserves an audience, an attentive one, even if not as rapt as we were in the early 1950s. We need the confidence that our story is of importance to others. Who these others are will vary with time and situation. There are our primary people: parents, partners (sexual and business), children, siblings, best friends. There are others at vital stages, such as medical, health care, therapeutic and social work staff. Sick people respond positively to being attended to, properly, and with the whole attention of their carers. That is: listening carefully to the twists and turns and blind alleys of their own unique story. One cancer patient said she felt she had been treated as if she was an 'illness with a person attached' (Petrone 2001, p.34). She also said 'this rather negated the rest of my life'. This losing of her personhood in illness did not help her to thrive through her treatment.

Patients do not offer generalised stories to their professional carers and healers, they present with their own particular one. It might sound like a variation on a theme to a health worker, but it is still unique. Well we know that: I know you, my reader knows that; you wouldn't be reading this book if you were the kind who treated an 'illness with a person attached'. Not that you are certain, any more than I am, that you are able to listen to every single patient with such attention all the time. What is less obvious is that patients and clinical staff tell very different stories to each other, use different metaphors or similes, and often have very different understandings of the same situation (Sweeney *et al.* 2001).

Each person's own story is the most important in their lives. It tells them who they are and what their roles are here on earth. We are rudderless if our stories are incoherent or unclear. We fail to thrive if we are telling ourselves a 'sick story', rather than a 'well' one. People's main stories change radically when they become ill. The plots change even more when they know they are suffering from a life-threatening disease or dying. Patients can be supported in reformulating their stories from sick ones to well ones, from muddled ones to strong ones, from negative and morose to positive and life-enhancing. People can be healed and yet still die. There are many accounts of beautiful deaths where both the dying person and their family and loved ones are at peace with the inevitability of death (Murray 2001). There has been much work done on this, and I will refer you to the excellent texts on how to help patients with their stories (Montgomery Hunter 1991; Brody 1987). My story here is about listening: patients and practitioners listening to themselves, to each other, and practitioners listening to patients; how to listen effectively, and how to set up the conditions for it – using writing.

The kind of close attention which is paid by a listener in a dialogue is an essential ingredient for all of us to achieve the physical, mental and emotional well-being that is our right on this earth. We are pack animals, not loners; we need this focus upon ourselves, this recognition of ourselves as unique and valued individuals.

There is one vital interlocutor, one vital hearer of the story, who is too often ignored, or not sufficiently respected. The most vital listener to all our tales of joy and woe and confusion: *myself.*

Listening to our own stories

If I can't listen to myself then I can't know what I want to say to others, and I can't begin to hear the needs and wants of others clearly either. It's a bit like the aphorism to which we have become so used: 'I can't really love others unless I love myself.'

If we can listen to ourselves then we can begin to work out what we want and need (or what we can offer), so we know better what to ask for (or what to give). So often we feel we are in a state of wanting, but don't really know what we want. Those who have problems preventing themselves overeating (or drinking too much), and therefore becoming overweight (or alcoholic) are perhaps a good example of this. They know they want, but they don't know what, and so they reach for the most available comforting thing – food or alcohol. It isn't what they really want or need, so they carry on overeating or drinking, in an effort to stop that terrible crying want.

In a gilt frame, on top of the desk above me as I write, is a print of a picture by the eighteenth-century visionary painter and poet, William Blake. It depicts a person just about to climb a ladder they have leant up against the moon, to the consternation of two onlookers. The caption, also by Blake I assume, reads: 'I want! I want!' I don't know what Blake intended, but I have it here because I think we all have an innate right to want. We are born wanting and we die wanting. That's what we're like, and it's OK. What isn't OK is a constant denial of want, or re-channelling of it into something which will inevitably be inappropriate or unsatisfactory.

It's OK to want because we also, and equally naturally, have a desire to fulfil the wants of others. There is nothing more fulfilling than to be in a relationship, whether professional or personal, where we are able to give the other person what we and they know they want.

I suspect the framing of this little Blake picture in *gilt* is an unconscious irony. There is so much *guilt* associated with wanting. And it's the cause of a lot of problems.

If we can listen to ourselves coherently, lovingly and un-guiltily then we can begin to create a coherent story to tell others. The telling ourselves can also be like a rehearsal to work out what we want and need to say, so the communication comes out coherently and intelligibly to others.

It's a funny thing; we are the greatest authorities on ourselves, yet we are extraordinarily deaf to the 'still small voices' inside, which can give the keys to understandings. Nobody can know me like I can know myself. Yet I don't, and I make little effort to try. Who's going to do it if I don't? Yet we really do think that clinicians *can* tell us what's wrong with us, and what we should do to put it right. What a topsy-turvy state of affairs.

What do patients want? There is little chance of clinicians, or other practitioners, being able to work out what patients want and need (apart from the physical needs which their clinical skill enables them to determine) if patients have no idea themselves. There's a saying in medicine: 'listen to the patient, they are giving you the diagnosis.' Well, the method I am offering you in this chapter will enable that patient to give it a great deal more clearly. And you to hear it far more clearly.

The relationship between a practitioner and a patient (client) is two-way. Both bring wants and needs, impatience, blocks to understandings (as well as skill and experience of course) to each encounter. Practitioners, as well as patients, could do well to listen to themselves in order to understand themselves better, and therefore manage their relationship with their patients more effectively. This is why I have been referring to 'we' rather than the 'they' of the patients. Though of course all of us practitioners are patients at times, as well.

This chapter, and my work in general, therefore, addresses itself to both patients and practitioners. Both can use a similar approach to create an effective dialogue with themselves.

Expressive, explorative, reflective creative writing is the best way I have found for people to begin to listen to themselves. (Bolton 1999, Bolton 2001, Landgrebe and Winter 1994, Winter, Buck and Sobiechowska 1999). When I say *themselves*, I mean that everyone has a range of different selves to listen to. Not only does the thinking me have a lot of different voices, but so also does my body, and the spiritual, and emotional me's.

Listening to my own story

I came to this work through having used writing to get me through my own version of post-traumatic stress disorder. I had been struggling all my remembered life, and one day my husband happened to say: 'Why don't you write your autobiography?' I had been to an in-service day recently in which there was a writing workshop: my initiation. I remember nothing about it, but that it was run by a woman, and the electric charge of the writing. Whether it was this that made him think of it, neither of us now knows.

I sat at our kitchen table in our cottage in the middle of nowhere, where we kept goats and fowls, and grew all our own vegetables and fruit, and I wrote. I wrote an idyllic story at first. Then I wrote another. The first one came out as coherent prose, written sedately at that kitchen table. The second was a chaotic angst-ridden diary: sometimes on huge sheets of paper scribbled in red felt tip, sometimes on tiny scraps in spider language. I wrote it curled up in a ball at the furthest corner of the house from door or telephone – tightly wrapped in the duvet, or in the window of a high-rise tower-block office I borrowed, sometimes hidden in a wood, or on a moor top.

This diary, which ran to several volumes of ring binder, I reread and reworked on parts to create poems. Writing those poems was a long and painful process, the understanding of what had happened to me dawning slowly as the writing told me – in images and stories and poetic accounts. In these poems I spoke in the voice of Little Red Riding Hood, I had conversations with trees, I spoke in the voice of one of Lot's daughters from the Genesis story. These voices, few of them my everyday one, enabled me to see, to understand my story. The publication of those poems was a milestone to me. I've still got a long way to go.

Much writing has happened since then, much understanding, anger, fear, horror, hurt, despair, joy, bleakness, support, and forgiveness. It's not something I will ever be able to leave behind me, nor understand how and why what happened to me as a child could possibly happen. But there is no doubt in my mind I would be a psychiatric patient if I had not discovered writing.

A further milestone for me is writing this section to this chapter. I had completed the chapter, and Christina, the editor of this book, very gently told me I'd missed out a vital bit. She told me where to put it, and suggested I wrote about why I do the work I do. Here is that section.

I never ask anyone else to do anything in writing I have not done myself. I am aware of the kind of support this kind of writing needs. But when people say: 'This is really dangerous, Gillie. How can you possibly suggest other people do this?', my answer is very simple: 'I know this sort of writing can offer understandings and relief to the extent of saving sanity. How could I live with myself knowing this vital fact and not passing it on to as many people as I possibly can?' My interlocutor always agrees.

A group of palliative care clinicians

The Northern General Hospital in Sheffield is going to have a brand new Palliative Care Unit. I am working with the palliative care team until the new unit is open, and for a while afterwards. I am encouraging staff, patients and relatives to reflect upon whatever they need to reflect upon – using writing as the medium and the tool. Bill's story, told at the beginning of the chapter, was written and discussed during a multi-disciplinary staff writing group. The project is still in its infancy, but I would like to share with you more of the stories from the staff. Here is some of this writing.

> When you have worked with a family who are struggling separately to accept a diagnosis and are perhaps not communicating openly with each other, bringing people to a state of open awareness is a joy. It feels as if a great burden has been lifted, for me at least, and I am certain this is also experienced by the person and their family. This probably sounds dreadful but it gives me a great sense of joy to check the computer in the morning and to discover that someone who has been dying over a long period of time has finally died. The protracted dying period is a dreadful time for all involved, in most cases, especially when people have been told that the patient is not expected to live overnight and has subsequently lived in a moribund state for

two to three weeks, with the family and carers riding a roller-coaster of emotion. A sense of peace may now prevail following so much suffering.

Less morbidly I get a sense of joy from many of the people I see, those who, despite all their suffering, will say, 'Well that's enough about me, how are you?' or 'Well I'm 80, I've got to die, I have had a good life', said not just stoically, but with a tremendous sense of peace. (Macmillan Nurse 2002)

This nurse was a little disappointed, I think, that he had not focused on one patient: told a story, as he did in other writings. But what he is saying here is so important for palliative care people to share with each other. This was reflected in the discussion.

The theme the group were writing to on this occasion was 'joy'. Bill Noble was unable to share the story he wrote on that occasion publicly, because although the writing of it was highly charged and useful to him, and the ensuing discussion extremely valuable, confidentiality made it impossible to publish.

This kind of work is appropriate in any health care and medical setting, but particularly appropriate in palliative care. Dying can force people to focus on important questions: who am I beyond this body, this person in a social setting?; who is it who does this thinking and feeling, and what happens to this self when my body ceases to function?; am I 'soul' with a body, or am I my body, therefore to disappear at death? Poetry, or poetic expressive writing, is a language which helps us to approach the spiritual, because it relies upon metaphor, on a non-linear approach to understanding. It allows us to explore the unexplorable, to attempt to express the inexpressible. If 'the spiritual dimension of palliative care…is the final piece of the holistic jigsaw completing the integrated whole' (Cobb 2001), then imaginative expressive writing can help us to fit this final piece into place.

Writing to be listened to

Creative, or expressive, explorative, reflective or therapeutic writing is primarily a communication with the self. I am here speaking of diary, journal, personal autobiographical, personal poetic writing. A secondary audience of other readers is often a vital element of the process, but to begin with, the main readers are the writers themselves.

Writing and tape recording (audio or video) are the only means we have of listening to what we have said. But a piece of tape recording is *in camera* – locked up in the box of the tape recorder, encoded on the strip of tape, until it is played back. A piece of writing can be reread whenever the writer wishes, and the thought can be rephrased, or even the opposite said instantly. Writing presents writers with what they have said immediately in a concrete and work-on-able form. And of course it also remains on the page unchanged for as long as the writer chooses to leave it.

Michele Petrone, the artist who works with cancer sufferers, would I am sure tell you that the practice of visual art can also help you make this contact with yourself. And seeing his work, I am sure he is right. Art, in all its wonderful branches, is a great medium for enabling us to communicate with ourselves as well as with others. Of course there is also psychotherapy: the talking cure. That is effective, but reams have been written about its magic. I'm a poet and writer. So I'll tell you about writing.

Writing creates an object out of my thinking

Why would we want to listen to what we have said in this concrete way? Why not just think things through?

Because writing takes things-which-need-to-be-thought-about out of the writer's mind and places them out there on the page. It can give form to inchoate experience. It can take subjective experience and change it into 'something rich and strange'. It becomes an object on the page, no longer only subjective. And the writer is in control of this process of change. Nobody else is in control, though it takes some people a long time to realise this, if they ever do. They are trapped by an invisible audience on their shoulders dictating how or how not to write.

One of the hospice patients I worked with said: 'It prevents things going round and round in my mind'(Bolton 1999). Writing can put these things at a distance: it can make them other. On the page, they then become something with which the writer can communicate. Putting something down creates a sense of another voice out there saying something to which I can respond – as if in a dialogue. How often have I come across a philosopher or writer saying: 'I don't know what I think until I write it down' (Bolton 1999).

I can hear the devil's advocate saying, 'Why would I bother to go to all this trouble? So – writing enables me to reread what I've said, work on it and so on. So what? I can do that more comfortably thinking in my bath, or – more economically with time – while driving.'

The privacy and freedom of writing can enable an effective communication with the self which is difficult with the spoken word or with thought alone. This is not so for everyone. Talking things through, painting them or dancing them might be the best route for these individuals. But for those for whom writing is best, and my experience tells me it's many (once they have overcome a feeling that writing is only for the clever or creative), the very process of writing can enable a distance and clarity. It can also enable the expression of things which otherwise would not be expressed or explored. I think this is mostly because the act of writing is solitary. The interlocutor is not visibly there, nodding and listening.

But there *is* an interlocutor. Writing with a white pen on white paper would not have the same effect. Writing creates tangible footprints which can, and probably will, be read. But the state of interlocution is postponed in writing. There is no immediate reaction of head-nodding, smiling, frowning, grimacing. There is no immediate response of questions, affirmation, shouts or screams. The first interlocutor is the writer herself or himself.

Some personal writings are destroyed, unread by even the writer. It can be really important to the writer to do this. The very destruction is itself an act of communication. They are saying to those particular thoughts or images: 'I don't want you. I am going to get rid of you. And I am going to get rid of you violently.' The physicality of burning or ripping, burying, or flushing down the lavatory can be much more powerful than any mental attempt at banishment of a mental image or thought.

The privacy of writing

Writing is private, unlike spoken communication. Writers can decide, usually, who will read their writing, if this is to be anyone other than just themselves. They can decide when, where and under what circumstances what part of the writing should be read by anyone else. Tape recording can offer similar privacy, but those who do this have to be confident with the technology and the sound of their voice, or the sight of themselves as well, if video-taping. Writing is, blessedly, nearly silent, and involves very basic equipment. This privacy can enable writers to express experiences, thoughts and ideas with greater confidence and less inhibition than if they are conscious of the possible response of an interlocutor.

This privacy enables a depth of concentration. The story being told, or the set of images being described, or the dialogue being written, takes over. The writer goes into something like a hypnagogic state. That is a state not fully awake but certainly not asleep. It is a state of being able to follow something in a non-linear fashion, non-logically; synthetically rather than analytically. It is also a state in which contact can be made with areas of the mind that are not usually available in everyday conscious being. These areas are not usually available because they would interfere with the levels of concentration required for conversation, work, driving, or whatever. The closest I think I get to this state, other than when writing, is when involved in strenuous but not thought-engaging exercise such as digging, or walking on my own. I don't think it's chance that the poet S. T. Coleridge walked and climbed incredibly strenuously for miles and miles, and then wrote on mountain tops (Holmes 1989, 1998).

For this reason personal writing can be experimental; it can be playful and absurd, or extreme and angst ridden. It can explore seemingly incomprehensible yet utterly insightful images using some of the games beloved of writers and invaluable for personal exploration (Schneider and Killick 1998; Graham-Pole 2000; Sellers 1991; Wade 2000; Rainer 1980; Bolton 1999; Kelley 1999). It can use some of the different voices which clamour in our heads and bodies but to which we usually steadfastly, and at our peril, refuse to pay proper attention.

Some personal writings of illness or distress have been made into public documents. These can offer invaluable insight into such experiences. Further to this, writers such as John Diamond, in his autobiography through terminal cancer, make it quite clear how helpful this writing is to them (Diamond 1998).

Paper Whites is a collection of poetry and photographs by Ann Kelley (Kelley 2001). It 'celebrates a death and a dawning. After her young son's fatal illness, hope finally denied, she sets about reviving him in memory in the places they shared' (p.6). Ann herself says: 'Eventually I was able to produce a few words – to find a way of containing the intensities of love and sorrow. I wanted to make something good out of that which is dreadful. Hopefully to "cure anguish and cause joy"' (p.7).

A lump in my throat

This lump in my throat
is a stone I cannot swallow;
It stops my breath my speech
all my tomorrows.

I should wield a white stick
wear widow's weeds or at least
a black armband, a plaster cast,
bruises purple and yellow

or have one of those sexy bandages
around my naked shoulder and torso
like a shot cowboy hero. If I wore
dark glasses they would see I am blinded.

If I wore a hearing aid they would shout through the sorrow.
I will drown in shallow water, my heart is hollow.

(Kelley 2001)

The stability of writing

Writing keeps an accurate record. Writers can, if they choose, reread their writing immediately, or several years later; it will not change. This is very different from the recollection of a conversation. I can remember conversations where I have been certain I know accurately what was said. And the other person remembers equally vehemently. But his recollection is totally different from mine. I am sure you have had equally infuriating experiences.

Writing can be restructured, be added to, have material removed or altered, even be rephrased to express an opposite opinion or point of view. Writing is plastic in this way, unlike audio- or video-taped discussion or monologue. Alternatively the destruction of a piece of writing can have its own therapeutic benefit.

These are some of the reasons why writers can trust the process of writing. They can trust that they will not be laughed at, despised, disbelieved, or shouted at, as a result of the act of communication with the paper. They can trust that their reflections will be stored just as they were expressed and that they can return to them to develop, expand, or rewrite in any way in order to clarify and understand more fully.

This trust can enable writers to express experiences, thoughts and feelings which they would find difficult or even impossible to share directly with another. This trust can, furthermore, enable a writer to explore areas about which they are unclear, or unaware of before commencing writing. Forgotten memories or unarticulated theories can surface in the writing.

Several people have over the years expressed fears that the wrong person might read their writing. Such explorations are safer in their heads, they assert. And they might be right, depending on what it is they're exploring. One nurse said she took her journal with her everywhere, such was her anxiety. I remember two novelist friends telling me they have both arranged for their personal journals to be destroyed unread if they die suddenly. But they were not terribly worried, certainly not enough to discourage them from writing.

Creative writing is a physical creative act

If I haven't already persuaded you how writing can be a really useful route to personal or professional exploration, expression and reflection – a way of listening to yourself – I would like to add two more elements. It is both enjoyably physical and creative.

The hand moving over the piece of paper can be a pleasurable physical activity. There is something about the appearance of those words on the paper or the screen, under one's own hand, which is powerful and empowering. Writing comes from my body in a way in which speech never can. It's absorbing and innately enjoyable in the kind of way other solitary physical activities are. I enjoy gardening, particularly repetitive jobs like digging, and walking on my own; others may jog, cycle, kick a ball, ice a cake, make model kits.

And then you've made something. It might be a piece of writing only for your own eyes. But it's been made by you: a gift to yourself. You might decide to continue through all the stages of writing to create a finished product. These stages are redrafting and editing – time-consuming, demanding and often frustrating but ultimately exciting, as they lead to something ready to share with others. The creativity of the writing process, and the satisfaction of the final product can increase self-confidence and self-respect.

Inhibitions

Many are put off writing by their schooling, or their belief that the arts have a certain mystique around their creation, to which they do not have access.

Many practitioners and patients with whom I work develop gifted skills in story or poetry writing, in expressing themselves effectively, and therefore communicating effectively. But few would like their writing to be read any more widely than by me and a small group of colleagues. In fact I have needed to encourage the people whose stories you read here to give them to me for publication. Nearly all of them started out with huge hesitancy, feeling they could never write.

The product is important, however, but usually to a very small audience. One hospice patient was delighted when, after much encouragement, she did some writing. I told her I thought it was a poem, and typed it out with short lines like a poem. It was beautiful. It did something very important for her when this poem was shared with all the staff and patients of the day centre. The hearing of it led to a great deal of discussion and sharing of pain and anxiety, which had not been possible there before (Bolton 1999).

More from the Northern General Hospital Palliative Care Team

We eventually managed to woo the registrar in palliative medicine to come to a workshop. There is so much vital work needing doing, she was quite right in saying she did not have time. When she did attend, she found the writing straightforward and pleasurable to do, as well as enlightening, and the discussion rewarding and supportive. Here is her story:

> When I entered into palliative medicine, I wasn't sure whether I'll cope with the stress of death and dying, and what impact it will have on my family life.
>
> It is very satisfying, rewarding and when symptoms are better controlled, when suffering is eased – I feel happy.
>
> In a clinic I saw patient as a new referral, and sorted out his symptoms. On the next visit he felt much better. I could see a smile on his face. As he was going out, the consultant came and introduced himself, apologised for not seeing him despite two visits. The patient said 'I didn't want to see you. This young lady was very efficient and I would like to see her next time.'
>
> I felt very happy and awkward. Happy in that I had made it as a woman from a different background. I felt happy that the patient and family were planning a holiday together, and that I was able to bring joy into their lives.
>
> I feel joy that I entered into this speciality. I had a fantastic leaving 'do' in Chesterfield when I changed my job, and received cards from my patients in whose care I had been involved. They sent me cards saying 'sorry you are leaving'. I felt sad but was also rejoicing the fact that my input had some value. I recharge myself from my experience.
> (Palliative Care Registrar 2002)

This is a celebration of having made the right life career decision, a celebration of the power and satisfaction of palliative care. To be surrounded with death and dying, and not only to feel this and express it so clearly and lovingly, but to be able to share it with colleagues is an enormous benefit to professional development.

Be bold

The wonderful thing about writing is its plasticity. Expressive, explorative, reflective creative writing needs this sort of boldness. The boldness is based on trust in the process of writing. When I write my journal or personal poetry, it's for me, or perhaps very occasionally for a couple of other people as well. I can say what I like, when and how I like.

The boldness this sort of writing requires is also based on a faith in myself. A faith that I can do it just as anyone else can. This in its turn is based on a generosity to myself. This is more than giving myself the gift of a bit of time, materials and focused attention upon a solitary activity. It is more than putting on one side the sense of my own inadequacy. It is a willingness to believe (or perhaps a willingness to suspend my disbelief) that all those different voices in me are saying things on the page that are always all right. They're mine. They're me.

So, three of the bases for this kind of writing are: a trust in the process of writing; a faith in yourself – that you can do it; and a generosity towards yourself.

When I start working with people and encourage them to write, I often give them this:

> Most of our energy goes into upholding our importance. This is most obvious in our endless worry about the presentation of the self, about whether or not we are admired or liked or acknowledged. If we are capable of losing some of that importance, two extraordinary things would happen to us. One, we will free our energy from trying to maintain the illusory idea of our grandeur; and two, we will provide ourselves with enough energy to catch a glimpse of the actual grandeur of the universe.
>
> (Castenada 1993, p.37)

Endnote

Reflective practice writing for professional development is not reflection which is documented in writing, but reflection enabled by the very process of writing itself; reflective practice or self-therapy *through* writing.

I think that we live in a fragmented world. Stable forces hold sway less than they did. I am no longer just me but a body over which medicine and health care can take control, a mind watched over by psychiatry with, steered by education and monitored by quality control, emotions which are played upon by the media, and a spirit which seems to belong nowhere. Writing, over which 'I' can have control, can bring back a sense of a coherent self, rooting the mental, emotional and spiritual in the physical act of writing.

Acknowledgements

I would like to thank all the palliative care staff and patients I have worked with over the years; their generosity, creativity, love, and care makes the work far more than worthwhile. I would particularly like to thank the Sheffield Northern General Hospital Team, especially Bill Noble, the specialist registrar, the MacMillan nurses, Kath Hibberd, and Joanne Brody. I also thank Marilyn Lidster, Ann Kelley, Christina Mason and Stephen Rowland.

References

Bolton, G. (1999) *The Therapeutic Potential of Creative Writing: Writing Myself.* London: Jessica Kingsley Publishers.

Bolton, G. (2001) *Reflective Practice Writing for Professional Development.* London: Sage.

Brody, H. (1987) *Stories of Sickness.* Yale: Yale University Press.

Castenada, C. (1993) *The Art of Dreaming.* London: HarperCollins.

Cobb, M. (2001) *The Dying Soul.* Buckingham: Open University Press.

Diamond, J. (1998) *C.* London: Random House.

Graham-Pole, J. (2000) *Illness and the Art of Creative Self-expression.* Oakland CA: New Harbinger.

Holmes, R. (1989) *Coleridge: Early Visions.* London: HarperCollins.

Holmes, R. (1998) *Coleridge: Darker Reflections.* London: HarperCollins.

Kelley, A. (1999) *The Poetry Remedy.* Newmill, UK: Hypatia Trust and Patten Press.

Kelley, A. (2001) *Paper Whites.* London Magazine Editions.

Landgrebe, B. and Winter, R. (1994) 'Reflective writing on practice: professional support for the dying?' *Educational Action Research 2,* 1, 83–94. London: Sage.

Montgomery Hunter, K. (1991) *Doctor's Stories: the narrative structure of medical knowledge.* Princeton: Princeton University Press.

Murray, P. (2001) 'A positive death.' *British Journal of General Practice,* 424–5.

Petrone, M. (2001) 'The healing touch.' In D. Kirklin and R. Richardson (eds) *Medical Humanities: a Practical Introduction.* London: Royal College of Physicians.

Rainer, T. (1980) *The New Diary.* London: Angus and Robertson.

Schneider, M. and Killick, J. (1998) *Writing for Self-discovery.* Dorset, UK: Element.

Sellers, S. (1991) *Taking Reality by Surprise.* London: Women's Press.

Sweeney, K., Edwards, K., Stead, J. and Halpin, D. (2001) 'A comparison of professionals' and patients' understanding of asthma: evidence of emerging dualities?' *Journal of Medical Ethics: Medical Humanities 27,* 0–5.

Wade, S. (2000) *Write Yourself a New Life.* Oxford: How to Books.

Winter, R., Buck, A. and Sobiechowska, P. (1999) *Professional Experience and the Investigative Imagination: The Art of Reflective Writing.* London: Routledge.

6

Learning in Palliative Care

Stories from and for my Journey

David Oliviere

Introduction

> A wise man learns from experience and an even wiser man learns from the experience of others (Plato, c429–347BC)

The dot theory of life says that one's life is made up of a seemingly random series of dots with the pattern of the dots only becoming visible on looking back on them: the shapes emerge with meaning in their connectedness. In a similar way, I feel my life is a series of stories, some of which have been tremendous learning and turning points. These only become apparent on reflection; at the time, the dots get in the way too much to be able to see the shapes. Only later could I see the interdependence, interrelatedness and interacting components of the stories that form the base of experience.

Many of the stories that have fed my personal and professional development come from direct work with patients and their families and networks. But professionals also have their own stories of lived trauma, crisis, anxiety and depression through which they have direct 'user' experience. Professionals, as with the users of our services, have been 'formed', not just 'informed', as the direct result of deep personal experiences of separation and loss, living with uncertainty of illness, struggling with low income, bringing up adolescent children, caring for ageing parents, and facing the meaning of death, parting and the unknown. We sometimes diminish the value of professionals' own crises and personal challenges; I was trained traditionally to see discussion of personal experience in professional circles as a sign of weakness and an absence of professionalism.

The stories that come to mind in my evolution towards becoming a 'palliator' (Clark 2000) are linked with my personal losses and those of clients in my first palliative care post. In retrospect, I realise they were landmarks in my journey in palliative care.

Attachment, separation, loss: my story

Childhood experience of loss

> Crying and weeping have been used by humans of all races, creeds and in all societies to express their deepest feelings...there are references to tears in the Bible, in the Koran, the Hindu Uphanishads and in every nation's folklore. (Carmichael 1991)

Born in the year Britain granted independence to India, the year marked a crisis for the established Anglo-Indian community of which I was part. Anglo-Indians grew in substantial numbers from the seventeenth century as a result of mainly British men's liaisons with Indian women – a practice encouraged by the British presence to form a mixed community supportive of the British raj. Anglo-Indians worked 'under' the British and enjoyed a very comfortable lifestyle. They aspired to be 'more British than the British', spoke English exclusively, studied British history and revered all things British. They occupied many petty civil service posts and middle-class jobs. The community is now aged, but there are still reunions held. With assimilation in their respective countries, Anglo-Indians are a sentence in history books.

At the age of eight, leaving Calcutta as the youngest of four children was sad for one reason in particular – saying goodbye to our family dog, Brownie. That trip to the station to board the train to Bombay was what I now know as a experience of unadulterated grief. I never knew leaving an animal could be so painful. The idea of coming to England was rather exciting, but I had not foreseen how hard separation would be from things to which I was attached. Brownie had been a close family friend and my sister and I howled our eyes out throughout the first part of the journey to London. Some years later, as a trained social worker, a psychotherapist would have had a heyday over the care I took to find secure homes for the pets of clients who needed to enter residential care!

I was always proud of the dual heritage my 'mixed' origin brought me; I felt I could understand the world from at least two perspectives. However, I soon realised that as a child arriving in London and growing up in its suburbs, not everyone saw race and ethnicity as something to be proud of. Diversity was little valued. On occasions, walking around the streets, was called 'wog', 'nigger' or 'chocolate' making it plain to me that I was seen on the outside as Indian. Even in polite company, to be asked innumerable times, 'So when did you learn English?' made me realise that people are blinkered by their own experience and that I would need to educate them. Not surprisingly, one of my main interests has become culture and ethnicity in palliative care!

My inclination to promote issues of race, ethnicity and culture in palliative care is directly linked with what I hope is a broad view of the importance of appreciating the uniqueness of one's ethnicity. It is impossible to understand a person without understanding his or her ethnicity and culture. Linked with this, I remember, as a small child in India, never really appreciating why some people (servants) waited on others who lived seemingly in the lap of luxury, whilst others lived in poverty. Looking back, I see the makings of the social worker in me, ready to identify injustice.

Then, as a child in England in the late 1950s and 1960s, there were few Indian restaurants, infrequent travelling to the Far East, little knowledge of other cultures and fears over mass immigration.

Adulthood experience of loss – cancer in the family

Sorrow that has no vent in tears, it makes other organs weep.

(Henry Maudsley, London psychiatrist)

I do not think my father's diagnosis and death from cancer was in any way more dramatic or remarkable than that of millions of others, yet it was for me a once-only.

I was working as a senior social worker in a psychiatric out-patient clinic in Nottingham at the time when my mother announced that my father was diagnosed with cancer of the floor of the mouth and would need to begin radiotherapy. Shocked, I spent the following two weeks thinking that doctors make mistakes and that it was not possible for my father to have *cancer*.

As the weeks went by, I helped accompany my father to radiotherapy and attempted to speak to the doctors to obtain accurate information. The struggle to get clarity from them on top of coping with all my own emotions as a family member was a beneficial experience. At home, I could not believe my father did not want to talk openly about his diagnosis and prognosis, although I kept giving him openings. Witnessing his 'denial' or healthy way of coping, depending how one looks at it, taught me how some people talk of things that matter or show their feelings in microscopic glimpses. It seemed odd that every time cancer was discussed on television, he would 'fall asleep'. I felt certain that he did not want to upset my mother, and I had to respect his own way of dealing with a life-changing situation, even though I wished he would be entirely open and expressive.

Subsequently my father had surgery to his mouth and throat, which involved losing half his tongue. Later hospital admissions are memorable not least for the attitude of trained staff who treated him as incompetent because he could no longer talk clearly, as he was now unable to articulate his words. On occasion, despite being told that he could *not* chew solid food, hospital staff continued to leave him solid meals.

For a long time I noticed that I was fascinated by how people cope with knowing they were dying, possibly a deep-seated fear of my own. I was intrigued by listening to colleagues who worked with patients with advanced cancer in hospitals and wondered how both professional and patient coped. Fifteen years of working in palliative care has not lessened my own fear; I now know that people adopt a variety of coping strategies and muster all sorts of resources.

I was attracted to palliative care as a chance to specialise in an area of work. Then, an opportunity to become involved with a new hospice being planned for East Kent appeared. Joining as a member of a new management committee for Pilgrim's Hospice, Canterbury, I served my apprenticeship and caught 'the hospice bug'. My next job move was to work full-time in a new multi-faith hospice as its first social worker.

Patients and their stories

Sarah and Pickles

> Peter Pan presented death as an awfully big adventure. Even for professionals, the road can bend in surprising ways.
>
> (Oliviere 2001)

One of my very first 'cases' on entering palliative care was Sarah, a 75-year-old patient who was referred to our hospice home care team with cancer of the lung. She had just been discharged from hospital and lived alone with her aged cat, Pickles; she had no family alive to our knowledge. Pickles was, in a sense, her only family. It was easy to draw her family tree. Sarah had extensive secondaries and gradually became weaker as our team visited.

Sarah delighted in recounting stories of her days as a dancer in the Windmill Theatre, a famous London night-spot when she was young. She appeared puzzled by her diagnosis and kept saying that the doctors were not sure what was wrong with her. She was told one thing and then another. Conversations were had over many weeks of visiting and on one occasion Sarah concluded that she must have had a good bout of 'flu!

Yet she was gradually deteriorating and the nurse and I were becoming concerned that she needed more help in her upstairs flat as she lost energy and was increasingly housebound. She only seemed to have the support of a neighbour, a young man in an adjoining flat. I was learning about palliative care rapidly and the conversations between Sarah and myself were going according to the textbook!

> David: 'So you think they told you you had the 'flu?'
>
> Sarah: 'Well that's what I thought they said...but they make mistakes you know...at one point they even thought I had cancer!

A couple more weeks saw Sarah take a turn for the worse and visiting from our home care team increased. I began to float the idea with Sarah of what would happen if she were no longer able to look after herself at home. She was resistant to the idea of a hospice and I let the idea ride.

Another two weeks saw Sarah deteriorate further and we were becoming quite concerned about her frailty and safety. I specifically talked about the local hospice and felt, as I had an excellent relationship with Sarah, that I could become more assertive. She eventually announced that the main thing holding her back was Pickles. She did not want to be separated from him and they had been together for 17 years. Indeed, Pickles had slept on her bed and was her only 'meaningful' relationship.

The next day when I visited, having secured a hospice bed, Sarah did not lose time. She looked at me straight in the eyes and said: 'You know who I would like to look after Pickles, if I went into a hospice?' I guessed that she meant me! I felt there was a real breakthrough in Sarah entering a hospice and being prepared to leave her home. I agreed to think about it and to consult my wife.

A day later I transported Pickles back to my home and Sarah was admitted to the hospice. I left him to acclimatise at home and he hid behind the settee. Sarah had said her farewell to her companion and I reassured Sarah with news of Pickles. When I returned home from work in the evening, Pickles was still in a heap, a grey, motionless ball behind the settee; after all he was quite aged and the departure from his home must have been quite traumatic. He looked depressed!

I made a lead and noose around his neck in order to coax him outside to 'do his business' and Pickles co-operated going out through the patio door. At that moment, in one gesture he freed himself of the lead and lurched over the fence out of sight. Three hours later we were still searching for Pickles in the darkness but he was nowhere to be seen! I had lost her 'family'.

What was I going to say to Sarah? I had promised to visit her the next day in the hospice and she would certainly ask for news of her dear Pickles. Textbooks never prepare you for what to say or certainly not the ones I read.

I arrived at the hospice not sure what I was going to say or how to explain that I had lost her dearest companion.

Sarah's first question to me smilingly was: 'How's Pickles?'

I paused and announced: 'Fine…fine'.

Sarah: 'What's he eating?'

David: 'He likes Whiskas…'

Once the lie began, it was difficult to say anything else. I had never lied to a client before and I rationalised that Sarah had only a few days, maybe weeks, to live.

Sarah lived another three months in the hospice. Every time I visited she enquired about Pickles and I reassured her that he was 'fine'. On one occasion when I was having some annual leave, she wanted to know who would feed Pickles and I reassured her confidently that a neighbour was in attendance.

I was sad when Sarah died. I had done a lot of work with her and I had become 'honorary family'. After seeing her laid out at the hospice and having said my goodbyes to her, I returned to our home care team offices. My colleagues joked and said that Sarah would now know where Pickles really was, pointing to heaven!

At the hospice we offered a bereavement follow-up visit to relatives and close friends of deceased patients six weeks after the death. This was very much the province of the social work department. There was no-one to visit in Sarah's case, but I communicated with the young man, a neighbour of Sarah's. I thanked him for all the support he had given Sarah. Before saying goodbye, he asked me: 'By the way, whatever did happen to Pickles? Because when I visited Sarah in the hospice, she kept saying, "There must be something going on because every time I ask about Pickles, David goes funny"'.

On reflection, the learning from this early 'case' was immense.

- I learned that you communicate with people without opening your mouth; patients pick up subtle messages; people read your face and body language. It is difficult to lie.

- Although an experienced social worker, as I began this work in hospice and palliative care, my professional boundaries began to become permeable. Issues that are relatively impervious in other settings begin to blur the boundaries between the personal and professional. I have found this with a number of professionals in palliative care – even the most experienced will act in a way they would not do otherwise.

- As I became clouded and drawn into feeling that I was the only one to 'sort' the situation and rescue this client, I made less use of my team, a vital resource in palliative care. If I had shared more of my dilemmas with the team, they may have helped me find other solutions.

- Working in relative isolation, I did not stop to explore the alternatives, e.g. a neighbour to care for the cat.

- Unethical behaviour has a ripple effect. In this case, we do not know how many other worries Sarah accumulated as a result of picking up that 'something was wrong'.

This experience raised fundamental issues over truth-telling, honesty between professional and patient, power imbalances and professional authority. I had information which Sarah did not possess. I did not treat her as a whole person.

It is sometimes said that patients and families are the best teachers (Oliviere, Hargreaves and Monroe 1998). I shall never forget Sarah; she has travelled with me in lectures given in different places, and her story has, I hope, helped others to consider key issues in working in palliative care. Her situation resurrected for me the issues of pets, openness and cancer, and fondness. All of my life was there before me.

The Berger family

Your pain is the breaking of the shell that encases your understanding (Gibran 1926)

Families teach us so much. Each family shows us something different. Despite training, a theoretical and value base, and experience, nobody tells you what to do in a particular situation. And people are full of surprises. Sometimes this is more evident when working with children, as I found out when working with the Berger children. I learned with them and from them, every step of the way.

Joseph, a 42-year-old, was referred to our home care service with extensive cancer in the abdomen by his GP. Our nurse made a home visit to make an assessment. She found that Joseph's wife, Annie, was experiencing a lot of stress and that the couple had three children: Paul, 12; Claire, 10 and Clive, 5. The nurse asked me to get in touch with Annie, which I did by phone. Annie was coping in her way, but was caring for her husband and three children with little support available from extended family or friends. She was clearly tired and now the children were adding to the strain. There were several temper tantrums and Claire had recently written an angry letter to her parents saying she wanted to leave home, which had distressed Annie. Paul's asthma had become a lot worse and this worried Annie. I suspected that the children were manifesting a range of psychological and social reactions to their father's illness and suggested a family meeting from the start of my contact, rather than beginning to see members of the family individually.

Annie made it clear that she did not want the children upset or told what was happening to Joseph. She added that she had never cried in front of her children, so as not to upset them. I picked up clues as to what might have been going on in this family in terms of communication. I pursued the idea of a family meeting and made an appointment. I felt I was taking a risk, not having met them before, but I was working closely with the nurses who were building up a trusting relationship with the Bergers.

When I arrived at their home Annie informed me that Joseph was not feeling at all well. He was still in bed. The children were around. I had to decide whether to try and pursue a family meeting with those who were available. Working in a patient's home brings its own challenges over rights and authority. I did not know this family, but sensed I needed to take a risk and see how far I could go. I asked confidently, not feeling too confident inside, if Annie could go up and ask Joseph if he could come down to talk a little together as a family. I felt that it was important to structure what was going on and to be directive, giving clear instructions to compensate for what I sensed as a degree of 'out of controlness' in this home. I also knew that clients do not do things if they really do not wish to and that Joseph would stay in his room if he did not feel able to come down. A few minutes later Joseph appeared, gaunt and slow.

We sat together in the room, the nurse and myself with this family. I began by saying something like, 'We know when someone is ill, everyone in the family is affected – I wondered how was it for all of you?' No one said anything. It seemed ages and there was silence. It is so tempting to fill it. I let it ride, but felt uncomfortable. Eventually, as I have discovered from sheer experience, if you allow a space something happens and that it is often the youngest member of the family who will open the way. Clive, aged five, blurted out, 'Dad gets sick at night; I don't like it, it's horrible.' This reaction really got us straight into the issues of living with a dad who was very ill and led to a chance of recognising some of the difficulties with which they were all living. It gave me an opportunity to relationship-build.

Joseph was able to talk very movingly about how lonely and isolated he felt because no-one in the family would talk openly about what was happening. The only person he could talk to without pretending was our nurse. Joseph clearly wanted support for his wife and children.

At the end of this first family meeting, the nurse and I agreed with the parents that I would work with the children on their own for a few sessions whilst Annie and Joseph would be seen by the nurse, who would concentrate on symptom control. The four of us would meet together from time to time, so that I could keep the parents in touch with the work I was doing with the children. I knew that I could do no meaningful work with the children without the full co-operation of the parents.

I had four weekly sessions with the three children, using drawings and additional ideas from a useful book by Heegaard (1991). The drawing was only to facilitate and to accompany conversation. It was not intended to provide art therapy or for me to tell the children anything, but rather for them to tell me about their experience based on the drawings and paintings. The Berger children were particularly bright children, but I am not at all sure that this automatically makes the work we did easier.

I asked the three children about their dad's illness and we went on to talk about the nature of cancer. I wanted to have an opportunity to clarify that cancer was not catching, that it was not their fault that he had cancer, but at a pace that would allow these ideas to mean something.

Figure 6.1 Paul's drawing of his dad's cancer

Figure 6.2 Claire's interpretation of the cancer

Figure 6.3 Clive's drawing of 'pseudomucinous cancer'. The bus seemed to express his hope that it could all be driven away.

I met the children at home after school and the relationship of trust was building up. I continued to talk about cancer affecting all the family and asked them to draw their family.

Clive's drawing below depicts the family – his mother with tears dripping down her cheeks. She had been adamant that she did not cry in front of the children.

Figure 6.4 Clive's drawing of 'family'

We talked about how their lives had changed since dad was ill; they did not get taken out much any more and clearly felt that all the attention was focused on their father's illness.

Figure 6.5 Claire's drawing of her and her mother

Claire felt strongly that life had changed since her father became ill. (Claire's writing saying: 'Mum and I argue a lot about stupid things that would not normally matter')

In order to be able to identify and help the children explore some of their feelings, I drew circles and labelled the first two 'happy' and 'sad'. They completed the remaining 'faces' using their own words.

Figure 6.6 Paul's 'faces'

Paul was very attached to his father. This activity provided an opportunity to mention that it was possible to have different 'faces' and emotions at different times and that these were all OK.

I was getting to know the children's concerns and continued to meet with the parents together with my nurse colleague. I explored some of the worries the children were feeling. For example, I used the phrases 'I feel sad when...', 'I feel angry when...' etc. and this led to very useful discussion.

I feel sad when
I see dad in pain

I feel angry when
I get told off for
something I haven't
done

I feel frightened
when I am left alone
outside at night

I worry a lot about
my dad dying

Figure 6.7 Paul's phrases

Paul's phrases were revealing and made clear that the children knew much of what was 'going on' despite their parents' reluctance to talk openly.

Joseph was still having major problems with his symptoms, but was unwilling to take much of the medication prescribed. His vomiting distressed the children. Joseph and Annie were still keen for me to see the children. They were acknowledging more openly that he was dying.

At the next session with the children, I touched on what it might be like when dad died. Both the younger two announced that 'Mum will feel like committing suicide'. I was not expecting this response at all and was completely taken aback. I know that children of dying parents can worry about the remaining parent dying and having no one to care for them. This seemed to be a major worry for the two youngest.

Later I consulted my supervisor, who encouraged me to hold another family meeting to enable the parents to say who would look after the children in the unlikely event of both dying. This was a painful meeting, but the parents did tell the children what arrangements were made should they both die. Joseph was deteriorating fast and he was able to voice his sadness at always having been ill as long as Clive could remember. He regretted not having got to know Clive better. Clive did not come near him as much as he would have liked and was much closer to his mother.

It was just before Clivetmas and we talked about how, as a family, they could create memories of moments they had spent together, even in the final phase of Joseph's illness. We talked especially about how the family could help Clive and Dad spend some time together and they all seemed engaged in this, suggesting Dad and Clive have some story time together.

The last time the nurse and I saw Joseph was early January. He was very poorly and he was aware he was about to die. He thanked us for having prepared the family and we reminded him that it was *he* who had wanted us to become so involved and that nothing could have been achieved without his wanting it. He was in control until the end. Joseph also said, with a smile on his face, that he had spent ten minutes in bed that morning with Clive. He added, 'that was the best cuddle we have ever had'. Joseph died the next day.

Recounting the story of the Berger family and reviewing work with them, I can easily begin to look at the whole process with rose-tinted spectacles. It was not as neat in reality. I continued to work with the family in bereavement, supporting Annie in adjusting to being a one-parent grieving family and with the children's anger that they were fatherless.

In the bereavement work with the family, Claire particularly was experiencing a painful degree of guilt.

This family pushed me to make full use of my social work skills. They developed my ability to push families much more than I would have otherwise done in order to achieve agreed goals towards the end of life. They helped me gain more experience of multi-professional working, using clinical supervision and in managing my own sadness. Some 'cases' stand out and the Berger family was one of them.

If ONLY

If only did not argue with mom and the rest of the family.
I wish I had a time machine and could go back in time and change
everything. I wish I could make a cure which fits all kinds of
cancer. I wish I had made Dad go to the Doctor because he
was having back pains but would not go to the Doctor. I feel I
we could have stopped the 'illness' if he had gone to the
Doctor but I don't know even then if it would have been
to late.

Everyone has something they wish they did---
or didn't do.

18.

Figure 6.8 A piece of writing by Claire 'If only'

Concluding thoughts

> The essence of the therapeutic process, reflections on reflections on reflections. As counsellors and clients participate within counselling together, they continue to reflect on their reflections, co-operating together to redefine problems, explore contexts and achieve solutions acceptable to the client. (Gunzberg 1994)

This has been part of my experience of working in palliative care and I hope the reflections and discoveries will go on, with laughter!

They say those who can laugh at themselves never cease to be amused. I have seen so much of the funny side of people's lives whilst working with situations of sadness and intense emotions at the end of life. We are told that scientists have discovered that laughter is the best medicine, i.e. people who laugh more have fewer heart attacks! Being able to smile and laugh is a great gift and colleagues in palliative care seem especially good at that. What I have enjoyed is being with colleagues who have worked in hospices and in palliative care teams from different parts of the world, strangers at first, but connected in a way through common experiences and through the lighter side of human suffering – Victor Borge described laughter as being the shortest distance between two people.

Finally, I have over time, believed that I can learn and contribute in 'bite-sized portions'. I cannot make a big impact or do it all in one go. Changes, be they with individuals or in the system, can be slow and sometimes sudden; we do not always have control over that. Yet we provide the opportunities and sow the seeds for things to happen. A final thought from someone who has inspired me more than most in palliative care: 'Large lamps can be lit from small candles' (Saunders 2000).

References

Clark, D. (2000) 'Research and Ethics.' First research and development congress of the European Association for Palliative Care, Berlin.

Carmichael, K. (1991) *Ceremony of Ignorance. Tears, Power and Protest.*

Gibran, K. (1926) *The Prophet.* Pan Books

Gunzberg, J. (1994) *A Grief Counselling Casebook. A Student's Guide to Unresolved Grief.* London: Chapman and Hall.

Heegaard, M. (1991) *When Someone Very Special Dies.* Minneapolis: Woodland Press.

Oliviere, D., Hargreaves, R. and Monroe, B. (1998) *Good Practices in Palliative Care: A Psychosocial Perspective.* Aldershot: Arena Ashgate.

Oliviere, D. (2001) Unpublished talk given to Palliative Care Conference.

Saunders, C. (2000) Plenary address to the Annual Conference of the Association of Hospice and Specialist Palliative Care Social Workers. University of Surrey.

7

Accompanying the Dying

The Spiritual Perspective

Lois Pollock

Introduction

Dying is a unique, individual, personal experience for both the person who is in essence dying and his or her companions. There is no prescription for being with the dying: to accompany the dying is to embark on a spiritual journey of one's own and to share part of that route with another.

At the beginning of the year 2000 I resigned from my hospice post to take a year out as volunteer to a small Mallorcan charity, Friends of the Hospice, which has been at the forefront of the development of a hospice programme on that Spanish island. Having previously facilitated a workshop there on death and dying, for professionals, I was asked to assist in the development of a bereavement service. I wanted also to return to Romania in order to continue some teaching work for staff caring for children living with AIDS. My other equally important motive was an urgent sense that I needed to take time out to reflect on the previous years of working with people who were dying. I felt a longing to create the time to process those experiences, many of which held such intensity and tension for me and at times had challenged my core sense of self and my spirituality. I wanted too to clarify within myself the concepts of psychotherapy with terminally ill patients.

Increasingly I had found myself considering the professional issues of practising as an integrative psychotherapist and the connections of that with the whole area of transition, the personal meaning for me, as well as the patient group with which I work, of the ultimate transition – death. In contemplating transitions, experiences that we all have throughout our lives, I recognise similarities with dying. I began by trying to link the transitions of my personal life and the learning from my earlier professions with my current place and being and way of working. I somehow felt that by pursuing those threads, I would clarify for myself a method of practice.

Early years on the journey

I was born in Australia and left school following matriculation in 1963. My first job was as an apprentice scientific artist in the reptile department of an Australian museum. Such a job title may sound very grand: in fact, it was mundane. I drew reptiles, in particular, a genus of Australian lizard newly identified from a habitat in the Australian interior. I did not find scientific art particularly creative: it relies on accuracy, observation and photographic-like imaging.

When I question what I have brought into palliative care from this career of now long ago, I think it taught me to be extremely patient, observant, and to pay attention to detail. By personality, I am not particularly patient and that could have been a great hindrance. But when, on occasion, I am apt to want to hurry someone along in the therapeutic work they are doing, I bring back to mind the images of the slowness with which I worked as a scientific artist and the need for precision, clarity and having to stop and re-draft.

London

At the age of 18 I undertook what was to become a life-changing transition and left Australia. I had $50 in my pocket, a one-way ticket to London and no intention then of returning to Australia. Later, I undertook my second professional training as a social worker. At the time I was doing this, I sat somewhat uncomfortably as a local Labour councillor in a deprived inner London borough. I was trying to integrate membership of a political party with advocating for the rights of travellers and the homeless. Indeed, much of my adult life has been spent working with marginalised people and this has included those who are profoundly ill with such conditions as AIDS, those who are disabled and those who are dying.

The motivation to advocate for those whose voices are not heard follows in the wake of a deep sense of shame that I have experienced in learning in England what had been done to the Aboriginal peoples of Australia. At times it has been almost unbearably painful to acknowledge my roots as a member of the white Australian group (mostly of English stock), responsible in past years for confining Aborigines to reservations, denying them appropriate access to education, health, housing and social services, denying them land rights and in many instances until as recently as 1967, removing their children and fostering them with white families. As a mother myself, I grieved.

As a newly qualified social worker in 1982, I went to work as manager of a family centre on a high-rise, high-density housing estate in a south London borough. There I found a large number of people sharing atrocious housing with cockroaches, rats and ants. Despite the many problems, most families attempted to bring up their children to believe that inequality and injustice could be overcome. It was in the centre that I began my first therapy group with four men and three women – all of whom had experienced varying degrees of social and familial deprivation including abuse, and who had in turn abused.

In 1989 I moved into specialist work with clients who were affected by HIV. Thus began a further transition in my life and for 12 years I worked in a number of different contexts with people experiencing a life-threatening illness and with the bereaved. During the first year or so, more than 250 of my clients died and this had an enormously powerful effect in making me consider my own mortality. Also at about the same time, I met an Iranian man who was living with AIDS. He taught me what it meant to love and the importance within loving of learning to live each day and to be prepared to let go in order to be free.

The paraphrased words of a Sanskrit verse have been important to me ever since:

Look to this day, for it is the very life of life.
Yesterday is only a dream and tomorrow but a vision,
But today well-lived makes every yesterday a dream of happiness
And every tomorrow a vision of hope.

Until he died, that Iranian man and I shared a spiritual and personal journey that has profoundly affected the way in which I practice, both as a social worker and as a therapist.

Journeys and spirituality

The start of any journey necessitates leave-taking, of home, of familiar environment and the loss of structure that provides order and the boundary lines of our universe. After moving away from the familiar, the emotional impact of loss generally follows. Chandler (1999) likens this experience to a microcosm of the way that grief is encountered.

There are different choices each of us can make at this juncture, avoidance of pain being one. What I have learned as a counter-response to attempting to avoid the pain associated with transition, loss and grief, is to sit with the emptiness. This emptiness is analogous to wandering in an inner wilderness where it sometimes has seemed that there were no solutions to the aloneness, the profound sense of anxiety and the feelings of helplessness, other than to confront the existential issues of the meaning of life, death and the end of life. When I have allowed it, the stillness of that space has enabled a creativity of expression through writing poetry and prose. I have been able really to listen to and appreciate music, and to read words that I had previously skimmed over thoughtlessly. In this space I have felt truly engaged and connected with an infinite source, and also with my fellow human beings. I understand this powerful sense of connectedness and integration as the 'I – Thou' relationship that Buber (1958) describes.

People who know that they are dying have sometimes shared similar feelings with me – such as a man, a dear friend, who died at the beginning of 1990. He wrote of the tension and paradox of living with AIDS, and rather than becoming a victim, using his diagnosis positively.

> Of course there have been hard times. I have gone through a lot of loneliness and despair and grief of all sorts. But I know…when I am able to shout, 'Oh my God, this is awful, I have been abandoned and I am on my own', then fear subsides and faith and hope emerge…faith emerges out of my discharging anger and fear and I have sensed a tremendous feeling that everything is all right in the universe. (Sheldrick 1990)

And as van Deurzen-Smith (1997, p.123) puts it: 'the spiritual dimension in our world – can be referred to that of the Uberwelt, the world above…where all the rest of our experience is put into context.'

Graham's story

At the age of 57, Graham was diagnosed with cancer of the colon and he underwent extensive surgery and chemotherapy. He was determined that he would 'beat' the cancer, although the signs were not optimistic. He was referred to the hospice where I worked as a Principal Social Worker when liver secondaries were diagnosed and at about the time he had been offered further chemotherapy treatment.

Graham was very fearful of experiencing debilitating effects of further chemotherapy. He also expressed a fear of dying. He lived with his partner of 25 years, a man who could not talk at all about cancer and whose own sister had died of motor neurone disease. The partner would become quite angry with Graham when he voiced doubts about continuing treatment, or talked about organising a will and settling his financial affairs.

When I first met Graham he talked at length about his diagnosis, his fears of what the new treatment might cause his body to do, his determination to carry on working – even if from home – and a lot about his relationships, with his elderly mother living several hundred miles away, with his partner and with friends who had died.

Graham cried a great deal in that first meeting, but agreed that that was not a 'bad thing' and that he would like to see me again the following week. Three days later, he telephoned me and cancelled our appointment saying that he had felt very ill after speaking with me and had been unable to stop crying. He felt that I had made him cry! We did meet again and continued to do so on a weekly basis. Very often Graham did cry as he spoke about the rejection he had felt from his parents when as a teenager he had told them that he was gay, by the rejection he had felt when his partner began seeing a mutual friend and by the rejection he had felt from the church when he had told a priest about his sexual orientation.

Believing, as I do, that one of the fundamental needs of all human beings is to be in relationship, it was important to be with Graham while he attempted to resolve some of his past conflicts with parents, to find a way of sharing his pain at what was happening in his current relationship and to dispel the myth that he was somehow unacceptable to God because he was gay.

My tasks were to listen and to hear – to encourage him to find the words he needed to speak to his mother – to tell her how much it had hurt when she took him to see a psychiatrist after he had told her he was gay and to tell her that in spite of the hurt and her seeming inability to be with him now in his anguish as he contemplated his death, that he loved her. One day he asked if I would be with him while he spoke with his partner about what was happening to him physically and how much he wanted his partner to care for him at home until he died. I was afraid from the little I knew of his partner that he would be unable to respond to Graham's request and needs and so I asked him how he would feel if that were the case. He replied that he would be hurt, but he needed to ask for what he wanted anyway, as it was he who was dying.

Graham and I covered a lot of ground in a few months and when he was admitted as an inpatient to the hospice because his symptoms were not controlled at home and his partner was unable to care for him, he said to me one day, 'I have shared with you, thoughts and feelings that I have never talked about with anyone. I will miss you when I die'. I knew that I would miss Graham also and I told him so. For a time we cried together, sharing an intimacy that remains for me as a precious memory.

When Graham came into the hospice, doctors and nurses were largely able to control his pain, but still when I saw him daily on the ward, he appeared anguished and said how much he wished it was over. He asked me what was the point of suffering? Was he being punished for being homosexual? Did I believe in a life after death? It was important that I really responded to his questions from my heart. These existential issues are framed as the kind of questions that many dying people ask and perhaps most of us don't think much about them until we are confronted by death. Over many hours, Graham and I grappled with the questions, sharing our beliefs, our hopes, our experience of life itself.

One day, a few weeks before he died, Graham told me that he wanted to talk about his funeral: he had largely planned this already and had discussed with his partner what music and flowers he wanted, and what should happen with his ashes. He asked me if I would choose a poem and read it at his service. He talked very calmly of these arrangements, but when I asked if he wished for a church service, his eyes filled with tears and he said that was not possible because he was gay. I told Graham that I knew a priest who I thought would be willing to hold his service. It turned out that the priest already knew him: they had met walking their respective dogs in a local park. The priest had lost contact with him three years previously when Graham's dog had died. The priest offered him the opportunity of confession and when I saw Graham later that morning, he held my hand and cried as he told me that the priest had, at the end of hearing his confession, asked Graham to pray for him! In that simple request, Graham had felt healed.

Graham's room in the hospice was continually filled with bouquets, cards, visitors and warmth and love: many of his friends came to say goodbye to him and on some days he was quite exhausted. Three days before he died, he asked that only his partner, the priest, myself and ward staff should be with him. He needed, he said, to let go of the people who had been part of his work and social life.

About 36 hours before he died, I was sitting with him, not talking, but watching him as he slept and trying to synchronise my breathing to his, as I believe that this can sometimes have a calming effect for the patient and enable a connection without words. After a time, he woke. Speech was not easy for him now, but he forced himself awake and told me that he had only had a 'wash and a brush up' that morning as he had felt too exhausted to be moved to the bathroom. A fastidious man, this seemed to concern him. Then he looked at me intently and asked, 'Do you know the origin of the phrase, "A wash and a brush up?"' I didn't, and he, the librarian to the end, took delight in explaining it to me.

Those were the last words he said to me: not profound: in fact, quite pedestrian. But I felt that they symbolised the long walk we had begun together a year previously and which ended with his peaceful death shortly after that conversation.

I wasn't with Graham when he died, but saw his body a few hours later. I didn't cry because I felt that I had already cried with him and shared what was necessary. When I think of him, I remember much that he chose to share with me and I am thankful that for a time we walked together, he on his journey, I on mine.

Rights of the dying

You may be thinking, 'Ah, but that sounded like a very easy death, what about when the dying person is expressing anger or rage; is very depressed and has given up and won't talk, or is in unrelenting pain. What then are you to do?' Partly, I would respond by saying that we must treat the dying person as an individual and as a living human being.

David Kessler (1997), an American palliative care nurse, has written an accessible book that he describes as a 'companion for life's final moments'. He lists a charter of rights for the dying which I thought similar to one that could be written for the living. In his charter, he ascribes as a 'right', that of the patient to maintain a sense of hopefulness however changing in focus that may be and the 'right' to be cared for by those who also maintain hopefulness even when the focus may change.

Hopefulness, with a changing focus, and the seeking of spirituality are pertinent to this chapter.

As professionals, part of our challenge may be in helping those closest to the patient to hold onto a sense of hopefulness for and with the dying person until the last moment.

Hope

Our lives are based on hope, and often individuals try to control the moment of their death with the hope of a 'cure'.

Tomaso was a 40-year-old man who from being completely well was diagnosed with AIDS after a chest infection was identified as PCP (Pneumocystis Carinii Pneumonia). His doctors successfully treated that infection but told him that his life expectancy was probably less than two years. Tomaso informed himself of some complementary treatments available through the use of Chinese herbs and determined that he was going to go on living. He sold his business and changed his previously workaholic life style to one of rest, play and combining traditional medicines alongside the herbal treatments and other complementary therapies. He sought a doctor who would support his own care plan and for three years, he remained physically well. That period of time provided the opportunity for him to travel and see friends in other parts of the world. When he died in his fourth year after diagnosis, it was with the love and attention of friends who had held the hope with him.

Sometimes I think as professionals, we may be inclined to see the dying person's hope as a kind of denial of their disease and situation. This, I believe, is either arrogant or perhaps, masks our own sense of helplessness. Of course the parallel feeling to hope for someone living with a terminal illness is fear: hope and fear are never far apart, but if we take away someone's hope, we leave them only with fear.

This is well illustrated in Greek mythology by the story of Pandora who was given a box by the gods that she was forbidden to open. Her curiosity on receipt of the beautiful gift was to open the lid a little, thus releasing disease, pestilence, flood and famine – and all the other tragedies of the world. Appalled by what she had done, she opened the box fully and released the remaining content – hope. Hope is thus a gift from the gods and as long as we are alive, it is our right to have hope.

By denying the dying hope and telling them that they must face reality, we limit our thinking: if we only see hope in the form of a cure, then we feel hopeless when there is none. Most people who are dying, however, see the value of living hopefully rather than hopelessly and that is why they hold onto hope as a companion on the final journey.

Hope is something to be protected: it should never be driven away, although the focus of hope can change. At first the hope may be for recovery, while later the person may hope for a peaceful death. We may hope that after our death, our children, partner or other loved ones will be all right and we may hope that there is something beyond this life.

All that I have described thus far has related to working with a London-based, mainly white and middle-class community.

During several years that I spent working with the African community in London (mainly Ugandans), the most commonly expressed hope of those who were facing death from AIDS was that somehow they would be able to send enough money from their benefits back to Uganda to ensure the ongoing education of children left behind. Another hope was that when they died in London, their body would be returned to Uganda. This was because of a cultural belief that unless the body returned, their spirit would haunt the family in Uganda. During two extended visits that I made to Uganda, I had the opportunity of visiting a number of Ugandans who were facing death from AIDS-related illness and whose experiences and hopes were expressed differently from people of whatever culture and background that I had worked with in London.

Uganda has been devastated by the scourge of HIV infection; it has limited access to medical resources and the social services are sparse at best, and in many parts of the country, non-existent. Men and women I met in the hospitals and rural areas focused much of their hope on cure and when that failed, the most commonly expressed hope was that family they were leaving behind would benefit from one of the numerous small projects providing a form of self sustainable income – e.g. Send a Cow (a UK-supported charity that will give a cow in certain circumstances to a family in order to provide them with milk and income).

And then there is the situation in Romania. As in many other countries, it remains grim.

Many children born in Romania during the years of the Ceausescu regime were infected with HIV and an unknown number died. Following the 1989 non-revolution and fall of the former regime, approximately 10,000 children are thought to be living with HIV infection or with AIDS (WHO estimate). Over the past five years, during several visits, I have had the privilege of working with some of those children and with their foster parents through a charity, Health AID Romania. In March 2001 I went to Romania to do an evaluation for the charity. In one extended session with a group of children all with an AIDS diagnosis but living with relatively good health due to the access to combination therapy drugs over the last 18 months, they expressed the following hopes to me:

- They would soon be permitted to attend local schools (rather than being segregated because of their HIV status).

- A parent who had abandoned them into institutional care would want to 'reclaim' them and take them back into the family.

- Medications would continue to be available that would ensure their ongoing health and well-being.

- Many of their child friends who had died would not be forgotten.

- They would have opportunity to be trained for future employment.
- They would be able to have normal friendships and relationships in spite of their HIV status.
- They would not die before they reached adulthood.

The shape of hope is thus also determined by socio-economic and cultural expectation and provides a challenge to those of us who work within a multi-cultural society or who work in developing world countries.

The role of the companion may have to include not only assistance in modifying the objectives of hope but also in giving support as unrealistically focused hope yields to despair despite all efforts to assist in its restructuring or fulfilment.

Purpose

Hope is connected to our *purpose* in life. If you ask a dying person why they continue to fight to live, many will have good reasons for wanting to remain alive. Some may not see any purpose in continuing life as it is – perhaps they feel a burden on those around them or sense that the chaos of past relationships is beyond repair. It is our duty to help the individual explore and work through whatever is troubling them and to find both hope and purpose.

One man I knew in the hospice 'hoped' that he would feel sufficiently well and gain enough time following chemotherapy to complete the final months of his electronics degree course. Another man told me that he had married twice without divorcing his first wife. As he was dying, he realised that he was leaving immense chaos not only for the women, but also for his two young adult sons of the first marriage. Now that the truth had come to light, he could see no solution to the problems, which he had created both materially and emotionally. He had lost both hope and any sense of purpose in remaining alive beyond saying to me, 'I am glad that you are going to sort this out for me now'. He then fell into a coma and died, without any resolution for any of his family members.

Kessler (1997) says:

Purpose can be as much about who we are as about what we do. Our reason for being is not always tied to being productive. Remove one grain of sand from the beach, and the whole beach changes. Each person matters. Just by existing, we all change the world. Thinking about purpose helps people to realise that life itself is purposeful, and that there is a reason for everything. But the answer lies in the question, not the 'answer'.

A man I knew had suffered for many months with prostate cancer, lingering on in the hospice in pain. One day his daughter asked me, 'Why is he suffering so much? He has always been such a good man, a loving father, a faithful husband and a wonderful grandfather. He has held our family together through so many tragic events.' Perhaps that was part of the reason that the patient held on for so long; perhaps the purpose was so that he could receive their loving support and care. Or maybe his daughter needed to tell her father that it was all right for him to die; that they, as a family, would miss him but would survive without him, remembering all that he had given to each of them.

Fear of hurting loved ones is often a powerful force in keeping someone alive and I have witnessed many instances where, when told that it is all right to let go, the person has died peacefully. Indeed, shortly after that daughter's conversation with me when I had suggested gently to her that she perhaps needed to reassure her father that she and other family members would be all right when he died, he had asked to take communion with his family and myself. Following the short service, the patient then asked us to hold hands around his bed. He then said a short prayer for each of us and died peacefully a couple of days later.

Creativity and spirituality

It never ceases to amaze me how creatively many dying people express themselves in their last weeks or months if encouraged to do so.

In the hospice where I worked, patients were able to attend a day centre where they were encouraged to live until they died. There were many activities offered on different days of the week, but those that I felt touched me most deeply were the creative writing group and art sessions. In encouraging patients to explore their creativity, we enable them to express thoughts and feelings associated with living and dying.

During our life time we are shaped by our belief systems: for example, that successful academic results will lead to well-paid employment, enabling a life style free of material struggle; or that adhering to a balanced diet with adequate rest and exercise will free us from physical illness; or that modern scientific medical skills and technology will cure us when we become really ill. Inevitably, as life-threatening disease encroaches more and more, such belief systems will be challenged and fade and the patient will face the fact that she or he has to live with uncertainty and confront the probability of letting go of family, friends, financial security, possessions and status.

It is often at this point that someone will seek answers or want to believe that there is a purpose to life, perhaps to want to believe that 'everything has happened for the best' and that there has been personal value to living. Kessler (1997) talks of five stages of spiritual reconciliation: expression, responsibility, forgiveness, acceptance and gratitude. All human beings experience powerful emotions, some of which we regard as taboo and to be suppressed. One of these is anger. Toward the end of a final illness, many patients may question, 'Why is this happening to me? I didn't do anything to deserve it.' Sometimes the underlying feeling in such questioning is anger toward God and some people feel that they must not express that.

I knew when asked to visit a 61-year-old woman with end-stage leukaemia, that she had devoted much of her life to the church and that she was being supported by her faith community at home through prayer and other ritual. This woman had however become withdrawn and requested no further visits from people associated with the church. Her sister was concerned that she was 'giving up' and so I was asked to visit and make a psychological assessment with the possibility of referring her to the hospice-based psychiatrist if I considered her depressed.

When I met Margaret, she initially said little except that there was no point in talking. Nothing could be done for her; we could not cure her disease. I tried to draw her out a little on the detail of her life, knowing that she had been a respected teacher and had worked tirelessly within her church, particularly with young people. There was very little response from her and as I kept trying to initiate a conversation and feeling less and less certain as to my usefulness in being there, she turned to me and almost spat out, 'Where is God now?' She spoke with fury about her illness and how unfair it was that at a young age, when she had been looking forward to retirement and doing some travelling, her dreams had been snatched from her.

This woman was angry with God but had felt unable to express that to her minister – perhaps for fear of offending, or perhaps because she feared some divine retribution. We explored her feeling of abandonment by God at a time when she most felt in need of a divine presence. Eventually, I reminded her of Christ's last suffering and feeling of abandonment before he died when he let out a loud cry and said, 'My God, why have you forsaken me?' As I struggled to understand and feel Margaret's anguish, it was clear to me that she needed permission related to her religious belief, to express her anger and sense of abandonment by the God and faith through which she had lived most of her life.

Maybe it is only in expression – articulation in some way of feelings – that we begin to heal spiritually. The expression of anger may be for long past, seemingly trivial hurts; or it may be in the loss of aspects of ourself through disease or other causes, or it may be the loss of values that have shaped our life and sense of being in the world, but unless we express feeling, we cannot wholly move into a place of reconciliation and responsibility for our present situation.

An adult daughter asked to talk with me about her mother's advanced cancer from which she would soon die. The daughter wept and wept as she tried to tell me how she didn't want her mother to die and she didn't know how to tell her that. She and her mother had never had a close, confiding relationship, as she perceived her younger sister to have had. She had grown up feeling that their mother favoured her younger sister both materially and emotionally. As she spoke, the original purpose for our meeting to talk about her mother's progressing cancer and prognosis, changed to one of pouring out incident after incident of a jealousy of her sister and a sense of never being understood by her mother, but throughout her life, criticised by her.

Eventually, pausing for breath, the daughter apologised and said to me, 'That's nothing to do with what's happening to Mum now – I don't know why I told you all that.' Actually, it had everything to do with the pain she felt at not being able to communicate with her mother in the current situation. She needed to find a way of acknowledging her past feelings to her mother in order to really feel forgiveness and to enter a new relationship with her.

Summary

Accompanying the dying requires us to treat people holistically and as living until the moment they die. It requires of me a listening that is beyond the everyday form, an acceptance that however people decide to manage their dying, it is their choice. No matter how well we know the person, how emotionally close we might be, we have at all times to strive to remember that it is she/he who is dying at that time and not ourselves. My task in being with people who are dying, is to encourage, to help them to find hope where they feel none, to stay with their hope however I may feel about that, to be an advocate if necessary with clinicians or wider family and friends. Personally, my task is to look at my own attitudes to dying and death, to seek life-affirming rituals that strengthen and sustain me daily and to try and live daily as if it was my final day – to consciously attempt to repair the areas in necessary relationships that have become soured, to give love and thanks to all those who sustain and cherish me.

I mentioned previously my experience of finding myself in an 'inner wilderness' at times of great uncertainty or fear, and how from that place, sometimes I have discovered creativity. I want to share with you some words which I wrote from such a space, not to be read for their poetic non-skill but rather as an expression of coming through a place of anguish and sorrow following the death years ago of someone dear to me.

Journey Beyond

> In midst of domestic matters –
> fixing vet's appointment for elderly cat,
> part of present family –
> my beloved drew me today –
> insistent I come to gardens beyond.
>
> Fearless, I reached for a hand grown cold –
> human warmth gone.
> Sensed his transparency –
> unable to touch as in years long past.

I looked with awe, not sadness,
trusting his ethereal beauty
gracing a different space.
Aged wisdom, static words devoid
of life trauma – still beautiful and gentle.

I spoke of new love – found unexpectedly –
Of terrible pain and joy.
He knew, knew already of this, and a slow
familiar smile lit the face of love passed on.

He bade me allow him to wander
In space untroubled by illness and suffering –
Whispered farewell – 'Go in peace'
Reassured he would remain in my heart
Expanded by new loving.

(Lois Pollock)

'Death is a journey to be undertaken' (Barbato 1998) once; so it is for a companion, again and again.

References

Barbato, M.P. (1998) 'Death is a journey to be undertaken.' *Medical Journal Australia* (1998) March 16, 168 (pp.296–7).

Buber, M. (1958) *I and Thou.* New York: Scribner Classics.

Chandler, E. (1999) 'Spirituality.' *The Hospice Journal 14*, 3/4 (1999), 63–74.

Kessler, D. (1997) *The Rights of the Dying.* London: Vermillion.

Sheldrick, N. (1990). In J. Woodward (ed) *Embracing the Chaos.* London: SPCK.

Van Deurzen-Smith, E. (1997) 'The spiritual dimension.' In Emmy van Deurzen-Smith, *Everyday Mysteries.* London: Routledge.

8

The Loss of Children
Thinking the Unthinkable

Gordon Riches

Introduction

The effects of a child's death on marital and family relationships are profound. The enormity of changes in their identities, in their relationships with each other and in the worlds in which they live, are almost impossible to grasp. Only by experiencing this worst nightmare could any researcher fully grasp the depth of this challenge to sanity and to assumptions about marriage, to parenthood and to family life. Thankfully I have not – as one bereaved parent put it – become a member of this 'very exclusive club which, I hope to God, you never have to join'.

Nevertheless, the effects of researching how parents and siblings cope with the death of a child are also profound. Perhaps they should be. This chapter is a personal reflection on the ways in which working so closely over an extended period of time with bereaved families has allowed me to become an 'honorary member' of a very special and mostly misunderstood group of people (Riches and Dawson 2000). Bereaved parents, separated by a whole range of factors like class, age, ethnicity and religious beliefs, share one crucial thing in common. For a time – and in some cases, forever – they inhabit a different country, beyond that frontier that Paul Rosenblatt (2000) describes as a 'chasm' isolating bereaved parents from the rest of society. This chapter summarises my own journey, initially of the discovery of this strange and frightening country, and then of its exploration, guided by those parents and children who have come to know its landscape only too well. Inevitably, this exploration also tells the stories of some of these amazing parents and children who survive the deaths of their loved ones. But most of all, it also tells the story of my discovery of the dead – of those children whose lives, no matter how brief – continue to exert such a significant influence on the lives of the living.

The struggle of these parents to understand the deaths of their children taught me something of the meaning of dying, the value of living and the preciousness of my own family. Talking to siblings who survived the deaths of their brothers or sisters gave me an insight into my own childhood. In particular, their stories helped explain why having had a sister who lived only for a few hours, two years before my own birth, had such a profound effect on my family and my own identity. In facing death we discover the fragility and the wonder of life. In thinking the unthinkable – in facing not just one's own death (that is the easier part), but in facing the possibility of the deaths of one's own children or partner – life's priorities change. The effects of this research have indeed been significant. Personally, politically, and 'spiritually' I have been offered a view of life, if only distantly, from within this landscape of loss.

Zygmunt Bauman (1992) in his excellent analysis of the 'modern condition' argues that we who inhabit 'normal' society take for granted the stability, reality and endurance of the institutions and structures around us. As with many sociologists, he notes that these touchstones of our sanity are only a human invention and largely arbitrary. He quotes Pascal to emphasise the point:

> When I consider the short duration of my life, swallowed up in eternity past and to come, the little space that I fill, and even can see, engulfed in the enormous immensity of spaces of which I am ignorant and which know me not, I am terrified, and am astonished at here rather than there; for there is no reason why here rather than there, why now rather than then. (Bauman 1992, p.18)

It is difficult to confront death, even in such an 'academic' way, without reflecting on the question of mortality. It is impossible to design and follow through a method of researching such a sensitive and emotionally distressing subject without confronting one's own role in such a project.

In examining the work of other researchers, in reading the stories of bereaved parents and in exploring theories that suggest that death, far from being a taboo, has become a form of mass entertainment, it is impossible not to become impatient with a society sleepwalking through its own impermanence. This chapter therefore is both a personal reflection on the experience of researching death and an opportunity to note the attitudes of modern society towards mortality. Thinking the unthinkable has altered my past and the way I see the present. It has changed my relationship with my family and with myself. It has offered uncomfortable insights into the society of which I am a part, and a desire to see it different.

Intimations of (im)mortality

Often research is accidental. This certainly is true of my discovery that 'mortality' isn't simply an abstract idea but a lived experience that all of us, sooner or later have to face. Simply through collecting my son from a friend's house I came into contact with his father, leg and hip enclosed in a complex cage of wires and knobs. 'Greg' had been involved in a parascending accident. A freak wind had caught the parachute he was packing away and blown him hundreds of feet into the air, to drop him again and shatter much of his lower body. He agreed to let me interview him. Of all the insights that came out of his account, two were crucial for my understanding of the nature of death. The first helped me see, albeit at second hand, what mortality looks like at close quarters and how such a sustained encounter irrevocably changes the way one thinks. The second clarified how fragile a thing identity is, and how dependent it is on the roles we occupy.

Greg described a life and outlook that had been fundamentally and utterly changed. His view of his family and of his place within it had altered. His reference group had shifted from his family and business associates – with whom he had gained fulfilment and status – to his hospital consultant, to other traumatised accident victims, and to the culture of advanced restorative surgery. Greg was an 'expert' in his own condition and, along with his consultant surgeon, a 'pioneer' in this branch of surgery. He even accompanied his consultant to seminars on the techniques that were being employed to rebuild his legs. He had undergone, in his own words, 'a trip to hell and back'. He had experienced the process of dying and of being forced back to life.

Greg's description of two 'near death experiences' – one in the ambulance on the way into hospital and the other on the operating table –

were crystal clear and spoken with deep emotion. It wasn't simply the content of his story that caught me. It was the conviction with which he described gaining something incredibly moving and beautiful and then having to give it up again. The details of his memories were vivid: he recalled his 'insides being thrown together like a bag of bones' when he fell; his children crying as they loaded him into the ambulance and the siren wailing as they drove to the hospital. These awful scenes were replaced, he said, by an overwhelming sense of peace and serenity, of leaving his body and looking down at himself and his wife. This experience was repeated on the operating table. Floating above his body he felt miles away from the tangle of machinery and surgeons. Both times he felt he was forced back, even though he struggled, by his hand being firmly held – first by his wife in the ambulance, then by the anaesthetist.

In interviewing it is important to keep an open mind, neither believing not disbelieving the interviewee, but always respecting the account they give. Nevertheless, this was the first time I ever felt the hairs on the back of my neck move. Greg believed what he felt and saw to be real and emphasised that he would never again be afraid of dying. This perception of life and death being more than they seem in the 'real world' was the first of many I came across. Whether hallucination, wish fulfilment, chemical responses in the brain stem or a glimpse of beliefs that used to be more familiar, these intimations of the survival of the spirit undoubtedly offer comfort (some would say cruel comfort) to many bereaved people.

Loss and identity change

Greg described how, subsequently, his condition and mental state deteriorated during the many major operations that first saved his life and then saved his legs. He couldn't eat. He became depressed and, on one afternoon, was violently sick following a liquid 'meal' he had reluctantly been persuaded to drink. Just at that moment, another patient went into cardiac arrest and he was left 'for what seemed like hours' covered in his own vomit and unable to move. He said that his grasp of who he was at that point, already weakened by the trauma of his accident, collapsed altogether. Something 'snapped'. Greg said that over the following months he 'lost himself'. He begged the staff to let him die. There were tears in his eyes as he recalled asking his wife to bring him in a gun so he could kill himself. All familiar aspects of his previous identity – father of teenage children, husband, company director, sportsman – had lost their meaning. In one sense, the pre-accident Greg had gone altogether, replaced by a man with a badly broken body and a 'homeless mind'.

This account illustrates how being near to death and of being way beyond the limits of one's body affects identity. Yet it was Greg's 'return' to some semblance of normality that offered clues about how bereaved parents survive – though at the time I didn't appreciate their significance. Greg recalled being visited by a patient who had fallen through a factory roof and who had lost all use of his lower body. He noted this as a turning point because, as he said, 'this guy knew what I was going through'. Over the following months, he made acquaintances with a number of patients in a similar predicament and became close friends with his consultant. To be more accurate, he made friends with a consultant he found at a different hospital who was prepared to try to save his leg rather than advising him to have it amputated.

Another factor was crucial in the rebuilding of Greg's identity. The business company he owned included substantial building expertise. During his many months of operations and immobility, Greg designed, first in his mind and later on paper, a swimming pool that could be installed in the basement of his house. This major civil engineering project was managed and completed, with his wife's support, from his hospital bed using his company's resources.

These key insights from Greg's account grew into central themes in our reporting of bereaved parents' experiences. Identity may be extinguished or badly damaged through loss and trauma. Roles previously taken for granted and assumptions about the world may be badly shaken or overturned entirely. Nevertheless, most bereaved parents survive and, contrary to popular myth, survive as a couple. The experience changes each of them and often appears to change the nature of their relationship, but they survive. Some, eventually, even identify a 'legacy' from their child's death that alters the way they see the world and the priorities they hold. Undoubtedly, for many, surviving the worst thing imaginable deeply affects their sense of self and purpose. From our interviews, certain factors emerged that appeared to have enhanced this 'resilience'. Others appeared to get in the way.

Communities of bereavement

As with Greg, the support of other people who had been through similar experiences and their ability to offer some kind of guidance or reassurance was invaluable to many bereaved people to whom we talked. They offered a 'sub-culture of other initiates' into this new and alien territory. Traumatic events change and disrupt lives, yet some new meaning may emerge from the way relationship networks are forced to change.

The part played by The Compassionate Friends in enabling newly bereaved parents to explore with each other the extent of their grief and their frustrations is well documented (Klass 1996). 'Experienced' bereaved parents help those who are newly bereaved and, in doing so, find a point and purpose for their own suffering (Videka-Sherman 1982). Sometimes this ability to help others transforms into substantial achievements and career changes. Shelly Wagner, whose young son drowned, wrote a series of poems (Wagner 1994) – 'The Andrew Poems' – in an effort to make sense of his death and her own part in it. She achieved acclaim as a writer of considerable ability and her book won a prestigious literary prize. In the summer of 1997 I was privileged to hear her speak at the Second International Gathering of The Compassionate Friends in Philadelphia. She was one speaker amongst a number of eminent individuals – all of whom had lost children and, in searching for a personal meaning, had gone on to take up a career in helping others through counselling, therapy or psychiatry. Colin Parry, whose son was killed in the Warrington bombing, has similarly gained a new career and a reputation as a broadcaster and peace campaigner.

In that huge meeting hall or in little groups of two or three, in looking at the photographs, poems and written testimonies pinned on the memory wall, bereaved parents and siblings exchanged stories of their children. All kinds of loss were there: children who died at or before birth, toddlers, adolescents and young adults. Young bereaved mothers talked to elderly bereaved mothers. Fathers came together for a drink at the bar and shared stories of their children, of their inconsolable wives and of their own, often unexpressed, pain. People cried, listened, laughed, made new friends, and told of their tragedies and of their survival.

Dennis Klass offered the simple but significant insight that The Compassionate Friends provides a culture in which the dead can continue to live through the conversations of those who loved them. The outcome of grief is not to let go of the dead, but to find ways of holding on to them in spite of their physical absence. This was a truth emphasised in virtually every interview we conducted. It is natural that parents, to confirm and celebrate their parenthood, need to talk about their children and their lives. Often in our interviews, we would be offered a photograph album or a school report, and the tenor of the conversation would change. Despair and desolation associated with the death would be replaced with a sense of pride and fondness for the various stages of the lives depicted in the photographs. At times we could have been having a 'normal' conversation about our kids. Frequently they would interweave stories of their dead and living children. In The Compassionate Friends, these conversations *are* normal. Bereaved parents and siblings are free to talk in exactly the same way about their dead children as 'ordinary' parents talk about their living ones.

Outside the culture of bereaved parents they are very careful whom they tell. As one mother typically said, 'It's a bit of a conversation stopper saying "Oh yes, I've had three children, one's in the army, one is at university and one died of cancer at the age of thirteen."'

Professional support

The part played by 'experts' and professionals in supporting resilience also appeared to be crucial. Greg's disappointment at medical staff who, he felt, failed to appreciate the depth of his despair was similar to the frustration expressed by some bereaved parents at the support offered to them by counsellors and psychiatric services. For Greg, finding a senior consultant who supported his attempt to piece his body and his life back together marked a turning point in his recovery.

Andrea's experience was similar. Her twins were premature and stillborn. She had previously suffered a miscarriage. She felt that her husband found her intense grief very hard to cope with and her need to talk about the babies that no-one else had ever seen was embarrassing and unnatural. She recalled the care and concern of the hospital chaplain, who seemed to be one of the few people who understood how awful she felt. He supported her desire for a 'proper' burial for her twins and helped her create a funeral service that marked their brief lives inside her. Without his strength, she felt she could never have overcome her family's reluctance for a grave and a memorial stone and somewhere to go to visit them. Without the love and understanding of the maternity staff, of the time they offered them alone with their babies and of the photographs and mementos they provided, Andrea could not have recorded the reality of her motherhood or gained the memories to support this important part of her identity.

Re-authoring the bereavement script

The opportunity to channel his loss into something constructive was crucial to Greg's resilience. He felt that his ability to immerse himself in the detailed planning of his swimming pool enabled him to build an alternative future that not only took his thoughts away from his useless and painful body, it created a whole new meaning and purpose around his condition.

In our experience, it is not unusual for bereaved fathers to throw themselves into such projects, sometimes forgetting, in the comfort they get from doing something active, that they are leaving their wives somewhere else, lost in the despair of inaction and pointlessness. This is why the funeral and its arrangement are so important. They represent an opportunity to take back some control from the overpowering events surrounding the death. Tony Walter (1999) talks of the importance of 'writing the last chapter' and of *actively* creating a shared biography of the deceased person. For bereaved parents, the death and the funeral become, over time, part of that biography. Ongoing relationships – continuing bonds – with the deceased child extend that biography, often for the rest of the parents' lives. Building this continuing attachment is an active process and may be discovered in many forms such as in 'seeing the world through their eyes', seeing the child as a role model or gradually coming to recognise the impact the child continues to exert on the views and attitudes of his or her parents. Hence, creating a funeral fit to turn into a valued memory rather than just a brief black 20 minutes of sorrow is important.

The account that illustrates this best was the Tellytubby funeral that one mum and her friends organised for her toddler. They had music from the programme, flowers in the shape of Tellytubbies and an informal 'eulogy' that consisted of remembering the little girl's most loved stories and programmes. She recalled with some humour the stoicism of the minister as he coped with this strange mixture of TV pop and Christianity.

Taking time off from grief

In many interviews with bereaved fathers we came across this need to fill their minds with concrete projects such as fundraising for cancer or campaigning for leukaemia societies. A number of researchers confirm that this 'active' response to loss is a common strategy amongst men (Campbell and Silverman 1996; Cook 1988). Stroebe and Schut (1995) have described a 'restoration orientation' in grief behaviour. This consists of taking 'time off' from mourning and filling one's head with the practical problems of the future, or engaging in activities that offer brief escape from the role of bereaved loved one, deadening, if only briefly, the intense pain of grief. This isn't just restricted to fathers and brothers. Many professional women or women in full-time work also identified the benefits of the 'distractions' that forced their attention away from their loss. As one mother said, 'I would never have believed grief was so physically exhausting.' Stroebe and Schut, amongst others, recognise the value of this 'time out' from suffering.

Much later, after our initial research was well completed and the book away at the copy-editors, I had the opportunity of interviewing 'Rachael' whose entire family was killed in a road accident. Her husband and one son were killed outright, her second son died the following day – Christmas Day. To a certain extent, like Greg, many of the roles that made up her identity were wiped out in those two days. Her resilient survival owed much to the sustained support of friends in her village and chapel, and to the support of a skilled bereavement counsellor. However, at the same time, she noted, the chance to get away from being 'poor Rachael' – when the suffering became unbearable – was invaluable:

> After the counselling, I'd go into town and just wander, be anonymous. I'd stare in the shop windows, have a cup of coffee, and buy clothes. I have a whole wardrobe of stuff I've never worn. No one

knew who I was and I didn't have to explain…I didn't have to do anything.

Rachael went to stay with a friend in Spain immediately after the funeral. She arranged to be in India the following Christmas where, as she said, 'They don't celebrate Christmas'. She returned to work. Her colleagues knew what had happened but they didn't know her as part of a couple. She was a teacher in her own right and that role remained much as it had before her family's deaths. She recalled clearly the value of *both* grieving and of finding distractions from grief. Another widow whose grief I have observed over time echoed this need to fill her time:

> I needed to have something to do throughout the day. Each week I needed to know what I was doing and where I was going. The television was my salvation. I'd sit for hours watching old black and white films. And books…I did little else except read. They let me escape into another world…

The unique loneliness of bereavement

Nearly 50 per cent of the sample we interviewed for our study came from self-help groups such as The Compassionate Friends or Survivors of Bereavement through Suicide, and opportunities to attend their conferences and try out our ideas with them proved to be absolutely invaluable. In the early days of our research, it was The Compassionate Friends who introduced us to a series of couples and individual parents willing to be 'interviewed' about their experiences of losing a child and its affects on their marital and family relationships.

At the outset, I had not personally interviewed anyone about the sensitive subject of a child's death. This is maybe one of the reasons why the first interview with Jane – a local organiser for The Compassionate Friends – stays so clearly in my mind. Another was that she was able to articulate so clearly and in so much detail the events surrounding Samantha's death and the ways in which it had changed the lives of the rest of the family.

Though married and still a parent of a son older than Samantha, Jane's story helped me clarify the theme of loneliness that runs throughout our research and has given myself and my co-author the title both of our first paper and of the book we produced (Riches and Dawson 1996; Riches and Dawson 2000). This same theme was in Greg's account of his lost identity after the accident and it spoke of a loneliness that separates each family member from the others, creating an intense sense of isolation and disconnection from all that was once familiar and safe.

From a sociological perspective, this sense of unreality and disorientation reflects the breaking down of a fundamental trust in the way that things appear to be. Bereavement and trauma are like an emotional earthquake. The layers of routines, habits and assumptions we use to punctuate our days with – and which give life a kind of taken-for-granted meaning – crumble, so all our cherished beliefs are called into question. As with an earthquake, the landscape we took as 'given' shakes and changes and the very floor beneath us seems insecure.

Talking many years after Greg's interview with a man who survived a severe heart attack after undergoing heart by-pass surgery, he commented 'you don't take anything for granted any longer'. Another colleague, who nearly died following a sudden and undiagnosed kidney failure, offered the same insight – what was once certain, predictable and rational now seemed fragile, arbitrary and without logic or justice. Durkheim identified this state of mind as 'anomie', translating literally as 'without normality' – or cut adrift from the structures of norms or rules that make sense of our lives. Anomie is experienced as isolation and pointlessness, as lack of direction and a sense of being completely out of step. It is felt as a personal breakdown in the social order. Anomie is the result of being outside of the assumptions and rules everyone else takes for granted. To be a mother without a child is to lose the security of that raft of daily routines, feelings and behaviours that are central to motherhood. To be a parent without a child is to lose the future – that timetable of school holidays, first dates, college, marriage and grandparenthood that punctuate the 'parent' identity.

Motherhood and fatherhood are different in most cultures. Because each parent fulfilled a different role in relation to the dead child, and each parent had invested different aspects of their identity in the now lost relationship, the death affects them in ways their partner cannot understand, and often in ways they themselves cannot put into words. They suffer differently, they perceive each other's suffering differently and so find it harder to offer the kind of support the other needs. Often, it is as though both mother and father, having been scalded, in trying to embrace each other only add to their mutual pain. Life's meaning is built from the small routines, the details of the day, the caring tasks that mothers do for their families. Rachael said that after both her sons were killed, she could never make breakfast or sit in the kitchen again until she had moved house:

> It was breakfast time – before they went off to school – that I found the most impossible to bear. The empty chairs, the empty breakfast places... The silence. It was over a year before I could make myself a meal without feeling guilty about making myself a meal.

Another mother described how, together, she and her disabled daughter had defied the world and its prejudices. After her death, life held no purpose. Caring for her had been all-consuming, both physically and emotionally. Her husband had done what he could in the house, but worked long hours to support the family. After Helen's death the well-wishers' comments about her death being 'a blessing in disguise' confirmed her isolation from the able-bodied world she had left behind and faced her with the distance that had grown between her and her partner.

Jane summed this difference up in an example. Three years later, she still showed genuine incomprehension at how her husband and son only three months after Samantha's death could go and play cricket 'as though nothing had happened'. For her, the world had stopped. Nothing could continue. For many fathers, the cultural expectation that they be strong for their wives, that they continue to hold the family together, pay the mortgage, is experienced as a pressure to control their feelings and postpone how they feel. These different reactions are not exclusive to either men or women, and we found many women whose responses were, like the fathers, to 'get on with their lives' and meet the obligations of their continuing roles. Nevertheless, I will always remember sitting through an afternoon at a SOBS conference in Birmingham in a group consisting entirely of fathers. Each father, in turn, told his story of his son's or daughter's death. No one in that room would again suggest that men do not suffer grief as profoundly or in such complexity as women, yet I suspect that this was the first time any of them had ever been offered the safety or opportunity to explore how they felt.

Bereaved lone parents may suffer this isolation even more keenly. A single father who brought his young adult son home before the funeral gave one of the most moving accounts I remember at a conference. The night before, he said that he had sat by his side and read him the entire story of *The Hobbit*.

> He would never let me read it to him as a kid, so he was bloody well going to hear it one way or another before I let him go.

Family stories: a personal comment

I have been asked a number of times, 'How did you come to get into this field of research?' and the unspoken part of this question is '... and have you been bereaved? Is this why you research death or are you just morbid?' As a teacher of sociology I have always been fascinated by the way we structure our lives, putting whole rafts of routines, paper goals and symbolic certainties on top of the chaos that continually bubbles underneath. As a reader of Emile Durkheim I have come to respect the value of ceremonies, rituals and rites of passage that help create the illusion of reality, purpose, social positions and order. Here, at last, in the lives that bereaved people recounted, was a level of raw truth – honesty is the wrong word – that cut through the game playing that makes up most of our conscious living. Here was a search for meaning, a need to be heard and a level of suffering almost beyond the capacity of social ritual and cultural beliefs to contain.

The chaos and despair that a child's death injects into what previously has been an ordered and predictable world forces a crisis of meaning for many parents, especially mothers. I have long been interested in the ways identity changes over a lifetime, the way, for example, that marriage, divorce, retirement, accident and bereavement change the lives of those involved. The stories of these parents often contained evidence of massive changes in how they saw themselves, their partners and the world around them. Here, at the very beginning of this interest in death and its impact, the importance of talk and of creating a 'story' that helped put the dying and the life into some sort of order fascinated me. This theme has become a major insight, not only in my own work, but also in recent important texts from Tony Walter (1999) and Dennis Klass (1996). Conversations, talk, sharing perceptions of the death are crucial in helping individuals 'take on board', 'come to terms with' and adapt to very basic and fundamental changes in their lives and in the assumptions that never before had been questioned.

Only more recently have I seen the significance of 'telling the story' in my own experience of death and bereavement. Three years ago, in fact, when my mother died and at 49 I became an 'orphan', I began to perceive a pattern that I have only now come to piece together. Digging through the many things my mother left, I came across a book about a white rabbit called Tufty. I don't know how well-known this animal character is, but seeing it brought back so many childhood memories of being read this book about a rabbit who is orphaned, and who walks the frightening countryside collecting a range of other lonely creatures. He ends up building an orphanage that makes a safe and comfortable refuge for his friends. It has an orange cover with Tufty holding the hands of his squirrel and bat friend as they walk across this hillside. How many times had I heard this story? How deep is this narrative about loss?

I was not the first-born. My sister, Dorothy, was born two years before me and lived only four hours. She was taken away and buried. My mother never knew where, and she said my father would never talk about it. I can't remember how old I was when she shared this sadness with me, but I think I have always known it. I didn't talk about it. She didn't talk about it to my father. It was our private secret, reminding me of how precious I was, how unfair life is and how brave we have to be to carry on. It also showed me how men, like my father, have to be strong. He took the responsibility of not talking about it, of knowing what happened to Dorothy, but not upsetting us by mentioning it, and by seeing that life carried on in the face of such tragedy. So, looking back, it isn't surprising that my two closest friendships at secondary school and beyond were with boys whose mothers' died when they were young. This is, maybe, only co-incidence. And I certainly don't recall this fact having anything to do with our friendship. Strangely enough, I had been dating the girl who was to become my wife for a number of weeks before I found out that her father had died when she was four. How deep are these family patterns? What is the nature of coincidence? Perhaps I am reading stuff into this that isn't there. Either way, my experience of living with people who have survived bereavement goes back as long as I can remember.

I was very young when I first saw a dead person. My grandmother died when I was three or four. She was, as I understand the family story, a 'wonderful woman'. She looked so peaceful and happy in death – I guess laid out in the small parlour of her home as many were in those days – that my mother felt. I should see her so as to help me learn at a very young age that death is nothing to fear. I still don't know, 50 years later, if this acted as an inoculation against the fear of dying or as a symbol of the fate that awaits all of us. My mother used to take me often to the cemetery to tend the grave of her brother, 'gored by a bull' at the age of 14 when she was a young girl.

Looking back, death was very much a part of my early childhood stories. My secret sister who I shared with my mother alone; my dead grandma, at peace with the world; two dead uncles – the young one killed by a bull – the other, my father's closest friend and brother, who died from leukaemia, were the social ghosts that populated my world. So I learned a lot about death and loss. None of it was explicit learning, but woven into the fabric of family stories – as much what went unsaid as what was said. Death was a sad, usually unspeakable affair that produced sombre silences and knowing looks and enormous sympathy for those touched by it. Perhaps, deep down, it was these experiences that made research into death feel comfortable, familiar and important.

From the perspective of impermanence

I sometimes play this game with myself. Perhaps, rather, the game plays me. It began driving back from the first interview I did with Jane. She described in such careful detail the ordinary evening when her teenage daughter, as on many previous occasions, had got dressed up and left with her boyfriend and another couple for a night out. Jane and her husband – as so many of us do – had watched television, made a drink, put the cat out, gone up to bed, glanced at the clock, wondered if the kids were OK, drifted off to sleep. Then the nightmare: the phone-call soon after they had fallen asleep; her husband's worried voice; some information about a road accident, the unreal drive into the hospital. The night that began so ordinarily slipped into a waking nightmare, dawning with three of the four young people dead, her daughter included, with the fourth fighting for his life.

Sharing this shift of reality, from normal life into one where your daughter has ceased physically to exist, it is impossible, I think, for any interviewer not to recognise that many parallel universes exist. As I interviewed more bereaved parents and heard similar stories of secure and ordinary lives suddenly thrown into chaos, the fragility of my own world became clearer and clearer. Maybe this isn't too different from many parents who worry about the well-being of their children, but most are kept at some distance from the full implications. The generalised anxiety I previously sometimes felt about my family's health and safety could now be converted into specific and graphic examples. At the same time, hearing of these accidents and terminal illnesses and of the ways such trauma affects marriage, family and personal identity, I have been offered a chance to comprehend the transformation of lives from one kind of 'normal' to a totally different kind of 'normal'.

In this latter universe of meaning, death is real and immanent. Life is precious, but temporary. We all will lose someone we love through death. Others we love will too, one day – perhaps today – lose us. Seeing if not 'the whole thing' (because, as so many parents keep reminding me, 'You never get over it'), then at least I have discovered for myself what Rando (1991) meant when she said most bereaved parents 'survive'. That means the serious game of envisioning the world without my wife, without one or more of my children, plays me in detail and not just as a featureless horror. As I was writing the last few chapters of the book *An Intimate Loneliness* my mother suffered a massive stroke and, after a week of semi-consciousness, died. A year later, before the book was published, my close friend and brother-in-law died after relatively routine surgery. The adjustment of my own world to these deaths, and seeing first-hand how surviving partners go on or go under – and sometimes do both at the same time – confirmed how brief and ultimately inconsequential all our lives are. That isn't to deny the profound and shattering consequences for those closely affected. Rather it is to recognise that all of us die and that all lives, relatively speaking, are shorter than their occupants believe them to be.

The discovery I have made (although it's not new, for Buddhists have known it for years) is that death is normal and ordinary. It happens as often as birth and it happens to all of us. The mistakes we in the West have made is to believe it can be avoided. By turning it into entertainment (as in *Reservoir Dogs* and *Pulp Fiction*) and by reducing it to the size of news columns or the TV screen to be consumed as 'news and current affairs', we have put it in its place. That place, according to Bauman is 'sometime in the future'. Along with Mellor and Shilling (1993), Bauman argues that by quarantining the sick and the elderly from mainstream society and by stressing the 'youth' of older people such as Joan Collins, we come to believe we live forever. By hiding the dying and the dead behind the closed doors of hospices, hospitals and funeral parlours, the general population are free to hold on to the myth that death is the avoidable consequence of specific illnesses or accidents. Bauman's challenge is to consider a world in which we do not exist. How can we imagine being dead and therefore, not being in a position to imagine?

Sometimes I am offered glimpses of it. My wife, Pam, and I often take our dog for a walk at Carsington Reservoir. It's only a couple of miles down the road from our house. We have even got a season ticket for the car park. One of the more strenuous walks involves traversing the dam wall from the visitor centre to a toilet block half a mile away. At my age this is a useful target to aim for, and one evening I emerged to see that Pam had wandered down to the water's edge, with Bob scurrying round on the end of his lead frightening the ducks. Pam had her back to me, the sun was going down over the water and the geese were taking off in formation to wheel about and settle on the surrounding hillsides for the night. It wasn't too long after my brother-in-law had died and I felt, just for a few moments, this alternative reality. What if it had been me that had died? Here was Pam bringing the dog down for a walk by herself. What was she thinking? How was she coping? Had she found out how to get the petrol cap off and fill the car up herself? What about the lads, three young men without their father. What were their feelings? Which of them had picked up the burden of consoling their mother as I had done for my mother, 21 years ago, when my dad died? What about the house? Was she selling it or hanging on to see if she could manage it alone? Had she given up work as she longs to do or had it become a lifeline of predictability and security? And apart from these close family changes, what other consequences would my absence have produced?

I felt a wave of compassion as I stood there, for Pam, for myself, for our little family and the familiar life we all take so much for granted. Throughout this research I have come to appreciate and value the little un-sensational events in my life – like crawling back to bed for ten minutes with the coffee, curling around a warm wife before the onslaught of the day, coffee and biscuits in town on a Saturday. How many of the families I interviewed had experienced the same normality before their lives shattered? How long before those who were left behind could again experience some warmth and comfort in the bleak landscapes into which they were so unexpectedly thrust?

Perhaps if we listened more to bereaved people, perhaps if we even listened more to ourselves when we are bereaved, life would be different. Sometimes I have a sense of life slipping by, having to do things that appear so vital but which in 'reality' are totally inconsequential. It may be (on average) another 30 years or so for many of my colleagues, it may be next year, it could be today. I have attended the funerals of colleagues many times since joining the University, the last one only a few weeks ago. She was a bubbly, vivacious 32-year-old receptionist and the second colleague in two years to die from cancer.

The values of the 'modern world' seem truly out of step with the reality of our collective mortalities. If we really appreciate this fact, that death is a certainty, and could be just around the corner, would we spend so much of our lives acting as though personal existence is an infinite commodity? If I have learned anything from the accounts of bereaved parents, it is that very few things really matter. What is ultimately precious is all too easily sacrificed. What really counts is all too often overlooked in the pursuit of the pointless.

References

Bauman, Z. (1992) *Mortality, Immortality and Other Life Strategies.* Cambridge: Polity Press.

Campbell, S. and Silverman, P. (1996) *Widower: When Men are left Alone.* Amityville, New York: Baywood Publishing Co.

Cook, J. A. (1988) 'Dad's double binds: rethinking fathers' bereavement from a man's studies perspective.' *Journal of Contemporary Ethnography 17,* 3, 285–308.

Klass, D. (1996) 'The Deceased Child in the Psychic and Social Worlds of Bereaved Parents During the Resolution of Grief.' In D. Klass, R. Silverman and S. Nickman (eds) *Continuing Bonds: New Understandings of Grief,* pp.199–215. Washington, DC: Taylor and Francis.

Mellor, P. A. and Shilling, C. (1993) 'Modernity, self-identity and the sequestration of death.' *Sociology 27*, 3, 411–431.

Rando, T. A. (1991) 'Parental adjustment to the loss of a child.' In D. Papadatou and C. Papadatos (eds) *Children and Death.* New York: Hemisphere Publishing Corporation, 233–253.

Riches, G. and Dawson, P. (1996) 'An intimate loneliness: evaluating the impact of a child's death on parental self-identity and marital relationships.' *Journal of Family Therapy 18,* 1, 1–22.

Riches, G. and Dawson, P. (2000) *An Intimate Loneliness: Supporting Bereaved Parents and Siblings.* Buckingham: Open University.

Rosenblatt, P. (2000) *Parent Grief: Narratives of Loss and Relationship.* Philadelphia: Bruner/Mazel.

Stroebe, M. and Schut, H. (1995) 'The dual process model of coping with loss.' Paper presented at The International Work Group on Death, Dying and Bereavement, St. Catherine's College, Oxford, UK, June 26–29, 1995.

Videka-Sherman, L. (1982) 'Coping with the death of a child: a study over time.' *American Journal of Orthopsychiatry 54 ,*4, 688–698.

Wagner, S. (1994) *The Andrew Poems.* Texas: Texas Technical University Press.

Walter, T. (1999) *On Bereavement: The Culture of Grief.* Buckingham: Open University.

9

Reflections on my Roots and Personal Journey

Christina Mason

Roots

A bit like drawing a lifeline with major events marked out on it, I'm going to track some of the influences which have led me to be the person I am and the particular kind of palliative care practitioner I have become. Looking back on my life, I think there has been a search for integration for a long time; integration of different subjects, of formative experiences and, perhaps most importantly, of different parts of myself. But to begin at the beginning…

My roots are Celtic. I was the youngest of four children, born in Wales of a mother who was of Irish ancestry and a father who is Welsh. Wales is the land of song and wonderful singing and speaking voices – Dylan Thomas, Richard Burton, Emlyn Williams, Geraint Evans, Charlotte Church, to name but a few. It's the land of political oratory, rugby, leeks and daffodils, a monstrous amount of rain, and a language which is ancient and very beautiful. The politics, the language, the music, the games are all sources of passion. If I have inherited anything from the land of my forebears, it is probably this kind of passion, an important word, which has its origins in the Latin verb 'to suffer', and which is used to describe a particular intensity of feeling state in, for example, love and anger. These are emotions that are frequently experienced by people who face death and loss.

The early years in Wales were not easy and there were several important and clearly identifiable events and challenges, which have been carried forward as major influences on me, and the way I work.

Illness

When I was reflecting on my life in preparation for this chapter, I realised just how much sickness there was around me as a child. My extended family was very large indeed. Father had 12 brothers and sisters and my mother almost as many. People in school thought I was lying when I replied to their question about how many first cousins I had. Perhaps inevitably with such a large family, there were lots of encounters with illness and death: deaths of grandparents, uncles, aunts and cousins, a brother who was a whisper from death at the age of 10 with the dreaded meningitis, father being in hospital for several weeks following an accident at work, and mother who was most definitely unwell a lot of the time.

These events were certainly formative. From an early age I developed a view that death *was* inevitable and also terrible in terms of the impact it had on those who were watching their loved ones die and then went on to suffer the pain of loss. For me, unlike many children, the process of dying was not hidden and I was not shielded from the tears and distress and anger, which followed in its wake.

Hard as it may have been at the time, this awareness has had its long-term benefits. Because of my early experience, today illness and death do not frighten me, but have left me with a passionate desire to see the process of care managed with greater sensitivity and compassion than I had witnessed as a child. This desire was heightened by the experience in my early 20s of caring for my first child who was extremely ill and died just before her second birthday.

I think it's not surprising that I've ended up working, initially, in a large hospital and then, since coming to London six years ago, in a hospice. I find that I am able to stay alongside people in an empathic way and without my own fear interfering with their needs to communicate whatever is on their minds. I am able, too, to remain with them when they are in fear or despair, and trying to come to terms with the loss of relationships with loved ones.

Politics

We were poor as a family, and that experience fired from an early age a passion for justice and a search for ways to reduce inequality in society. Today, this informs the things I see as important and the way I think about social and political issues and the distribution of power – between men and women, different social classes and ethnic groups.

It is no accident that I have come to work in a hospice providing services for three London boroughs where levels of poverty and deprivation are amongst the highest in the country. Most of the people who come into the hospice as in-patients are on social security benefits and have no other resources by way of savings. The first struggle for the bereaved is to find the money to bury their dead. A substantial minority come to us from hostels. They have been living rough for most of their lives and have lost touch with their families. If they wish it, we will attempt to trace families and when this succeeds, it is wonderful to see the joy on people's faces as they meet after, sometimes, decades of separation. Sometimes, however, this reconciliation is not possible and the man or woman will go to their grave with only social worker, undertaker, and chaplain in attendance.

Often the most I can do for people is to treat them with the respect that is their due as part of their humanity. Perhaps for the first time in their lives they can be in an environment where their voices can be heard. That matters to me very much indeed, whether I am functioning as a social worker or as a therapist.

Spirituality

The church for me as a child was a place of security. I loved the cool stone columns and the colour of the stained glass and the way the light cast patterns on the floor. This was the place where I learned the importance of ritual and developed an awareness and acceptance of mystery.

There is so much that I do not understand about life and death and the process of transition from one to the other. It is now commonplace for us to observe that people, even when they are very close to death, appear to be able to exercise some degree of control over their passing. For instance, they will wait for a relative to arrive from abroad, and having said their goodbyes, will then die, or they will wait for a new grandchild to be born, and then go. And we have been aware of how, against all the odds and widespread disease, people recover their health and enter a new phase of life. Some will not be surprised by these phenomena and will attribute them to faith in a deity. Others will speak of 'mind over matter'. For myself, I do not know and am prepared to live with the mystery. The idea of the sanctity of the present moment helps me to stay still and not to get anxious in that great cloud of unknowing which frequently surrounds work with extremely sick people and those who mourn.

Education

1. Music

Music began to be important to me as soon as I knew there was something called music. I have lovely memories of running home from infant school to listen to the signature tune of one of the programmes on Children's Hour. It was the 'Dance of the Sugar Plum Fairy' from Tchaikovsky's *Nutcracker Suite*, and I sat with my ear glued to the wireless set, totally lost in the sound for a few minutes.

When I left school I went on to university to study for a Bachelor of Music degree with the idea of becoming a professional musician. Clearly this didn't happen and I changed tack at a time when my first child was desperately ill and I was trying to defend myself from anything that would make the tears come. I was afraid that if they started they'd never stop so there was no music for quite a long time after she died. But I'm now involved in music again and its influence on me is through and through.

For example, creativity and imagination are, I believe, as valuable to a good therapist as to a composer. Sometimes it is necessary to find new ways to help people to express themselves, especially when they have lost the power of speech, which is often the case if they have reached the later stages of motor neurone disease. Communication and relationship, too, are as important in music as in palliative care. If you've ever watched a group of musicians playing together you'll see the way in which a quick glance or a movement of the left arm seems to signal the start of a piece, or to play louder, or whatever. They are in tune with each other in a miraculous way. This is my model for good practice. My ideal is to be attuned to a client in such a way that I can give the response that is most in harmony with their need. Sometimes there may be discord and I may need to engage in gentle challenge, but it will be discord for a purpose, eventually resolving into a new perspective or way of looking at an issue.

One of the by-products of practice in music is that you gain fluency and, as you do this, you lose inhibitions. The technique then becomes harnessed to the music rather than the music becoming impeded by technical imperfections. Again, that is a goal in my work, to become less aware of technique and to be concentrating fully on the rhythm and cadence of the client's thoughts and feelings.

I also have occasionally used music therapeutically with patients who are finding it hard to relax and who are very anxious. The flow of music can bring a sense of peace. That is the way I now use music in my personal life, to bring peace and a release from tension. Singing in a large choir and beginning each rehearsal with warm-up exercises, my lungs inflate from the diaphragm and no matter how hard the day has been, I come away refreshed and invigorated.

2. Psychology and Sociology

While my daughter was ill I began to read widely in the human and social sciences. I think I was trying to make some kind of sense of things, to try and find meaning in this awful event and to understand why people were behaving as they were. It seemed like a natural follow-on when, after Catherine's death, I went back to university and studied for a joint honours degree in psychology and sociology. These subjects became the basis for my career from 1970, when I graduated, until 1989, when I left an academic post to train as a social worker.

Psychology has been helpful as a foundation for my work, but sociology, surprisingly perhaps, has been even more influential in my work in palliative care. The focus of a good deal of the research, which I carried out when I worked as a lecturer in a university environment, was on the subject of communication in health care systems and some of the factors that impede effective communication between professionals and patients. This topic is as relevant today as in the 1970s when the research was in progress. I also studied the way people come to terms with illness and make sense of the experience they live through. I became particularly interested in changing self-images and how new identities are formed.

The following quotation is from a study of delinquent boys, but it could just as well apply to any kind of medical environment.

> There in the cell for the first time in my life, I realised that I was a criminal. Before I had just been a mischievous lad…; but now, as I sat in my cell of stone and iron, dressed in a grey uniform, with my head shaved, small skull cap, like all the other hardened criminals around me, some strange feeling came over me. Never before had I realised that I was a criminal. I really became one, as I sat there and brooded. At first, I was almost afraid of myself, ebbing like a stranger to my own self. (Shaw 1930)

For the patient with cancer what is gained by the imposition of a diagnostic label is the end of often agonising uncertainty about the meaning of symptoms and the beginning of treatment aimed at curing or controlling the illness. But it is frequently relief bought at a price, the loss of a previous self-image and the necessity to structure a new identity.

'Doris', a young women I worked with, was very relieved to have found out what was causing the pain, even though it meant the removal of large sections of her bowel. She said she was well prepared by the doctors for dealing with the operation and the level of discomfort she might experience as the wound was healing. She also had a nurse to help her with the practicalities of a colostomy bag and she said this was a great relief. But, Doris said, what no one told her was that she would feel completely different about herself.

> I sat in front of a mirror day after day. Who is this person?
> Is she ill or is she well? Can she look forward to a holiday or does she need to prepare for her funeral? Is this me? Am I living or am I dying?

As a researcher, I was more at home with qualitative methodologies, and through extended interviews I tried to give people the power to tell their stories. The method is very closely connected with phenomenological inquiry and narrative therapies. Here is the way in which Richard Erskine describes the process of inquiry.

> Inquiry begins with the assumption that the therapist knows nothing about the client's experience and therefore must continually strive to understand the subjective meaning of the client's behaviour and intrapsychic process. The process of inquiry involves the therapist

being open to discovering the client's perspective.... This type of inquiry requires a genuine interest in the client's subjective experiences and construction of meanings.

(Erskine 1997, p.22)

'Gerry' was a client I worked with for two years before coming to London from Scotland. She was in her early 30s, happily married with two little girls, one aged three and the other a toddler. One September morning, she and her husband and children set out on holiday. They never arrived at their destination. An articulated lorry went out of control and smashed into their car. Gerry was slightly injured and was taken to hospital with mild concussion and a bruised knee. Her husband and two daughters were killed outright.

When Gerry returned home she was referred to me by the hospital where I was then working. It was my goal to encourage Gerry to tell her story from her own perspective. Here I want to emphasise *her* perspective because everyone around her had a perspective on the accident and the way they thought Gerry *should* be reacting. Gerry confounded everyone, however. She did not cry. She did not become depressed. She retained an active interest in her family of origin and her friends, even those with children of the same age as her own. As soon as her knee injury was better, she set about planning her future as a woman on her own.

I am well aware that some people may see Gerry as exhibiting powerful defences against the pain of her loss and that at some time in the future she might suffer a serious breakdown. That was a possibility, but it certainly would not have been sound therapeutic practice to undermine her defences. What I believed I needed to do was look carefully at my counter-transference with my supervisor, suspend any model of grief I may hold, and examine my values to ensure that I did not try to impose on her my own judgement or theory. I needed to accept that this was Gerry's way and that she may actually never grieve according to any of the textbook models. Working with her was a lesson I shall never forget.

3. Social Work

Another strand of influence on practice in specialist palliative care as well as on me, personally, is the training I received and subsequent career path as a social worker. All of the things I've already mentioned began to shape my practice in this profession, but there were two aspects to the training, which were new. First, there was anti-discriminatory practice and the need to evidence activity as an anti-discriminatory practitioner. Now, when I look at any issue that affects the care of people with palliative care needs, whether from the perspective of practitioner or policy maker, my judgements will be coloured by this framework. For instance, I'm sensitive to issues of prejudice arising from class, race, gender, disability, and other sources of exclusion.

The other important influence in my social work training was the emphasis on family therapy. This taught me to think systemically. I've always admired the poetry and plays of T. S. Eliot and the following quotation from the speech of one of the characters in his play *The Cocktail Party* illustrates well the need for the broad canvas provided by looking at systems as well as individuals.

> But before I treat a patient like yourself
> I need to know a great deal more about him,
> Than the patient himself can always tell me.
> Indeed, it is often the case that my patients
> Are only a piece of a total situation
> Which I have to explore. The single patient
> Who is ill by himself, is rather the exception.

(Eliot 1950)

This emphasis on the family is extremely important in palliative care. For example, partners and adult children often ask that the truth of a diagnosis and prognosis is not given to a loved one, although we are aware of the patient's search for accurate information. Again, we need to be aware of the exhaustion in carers who, having devoted sometimes years to their sick relatives, are unable to manage any longer, even when their loved ones are wanting to return home to the security of familiar surroundings. The single patient who is ill by himself is certainly the exception.

Gerry, whom I mentioned earlier was a case in point. Although *her* grief was not manifest, her mother, stepfather, sister and brother actively mourned and protested their loss. Sisters grew closer and mother, having lost her role and status as a grandmother, reverted to an old way of behaving towards her children that her husband began to resent. I worked with the whole family group whose way of being together was fundamentally altered by the awful road traffic accident.

Trauma

Another influence on me and the way I now work was a serious depressive illness, which began in my 30s. It was treated with drugs and ECT but there was no response and I remained low in mood, with fairly frequent dips into darkness and the proverbial slough of despond. Eventually, however, I was referred to a psychoanalytically oriented psychotherapist and from 1984 until 1991, I was in therapy for from three to five sessions a week. During this time it became apparent that I needed to revisit a number of events in my life, which I had shut out of awareness. Prominent amongst these was the death of my daughter, whom I had never really mourned.

Catherine was a very beautiful child when she was born and, for me, she remained so until she died. Apart from my brother having meningitis, there was no family history of serious childhood illnesses; nothing to warn of what was to develop. Catherine passed the normal milestones until she reached the age of around six months and then it seemed as if she started to regress. By nine months it was obvious that something very serious was wrong with my beloved child and an appointment was made with a paediatrician. It did not take him long to make the diagnosis of Tay-Sachs disease, a rare genetic disorder of metabolism, invariably fatal, and with a one-in-four chance of recurrence with every subsequent pregnancy.

Despite all the experience with illness and death I had had as a child, I handled this situation by closing down on feelings, and probably shutting down to life as well. I think my pride got in the way; people used to praise me and say how well I was managing. What they observed was that I was not crying or talking about thoughts or feelings. There was certainly immense distress when given the news that Catherine would not survive more than a year, but after the shock of this news I shed few, if any, tears. In place of emotion, I went further and further into a quest for knowledge, to find the meaning of life, why people behave the way they do, why did this awful thing happen? I still wonder how it would have been if I *had* wept loudly and cried out for help. When I took Catherine out in the pram, I saw neighbours crossing over to the other side. Was it the stigma of disease which I had caught, or was it simply that they did not know what to say? It was the loneliest time of my life. I felt like an outsider, looking in at the 'normal' activities of ordinary people.

When, much later in therapy, I did get in touch with the unresolved feelings, the process was frightening and I thought many times that I was going mad. And perhaps that *is* what happened, at least for a while.

After a lot of hard therapeutic work, I believe that I have reached a stage where no more healing is possible in relation to the death of Catherine, but that that *is* acceptable. I am able to speak about her openly and genuinely without the necessity to protect myself from 'breaking down'. I am able to speak of the love I had and still have for this child and that even with the pain of her death I am glad that she was born and that she gave joy. I have found a way of relating to this child that acknowledges her life and her death. But I am also well aware of my limits; knowing, for example, that I would not be capable of working professionally with children who are very ill and likely to die. We all have our Achilles' heels professionally, and this is mine.

The seven years of therapy were desperately difficult, but enabled me to discover hidden parts of myself and to understand why I felt so bad about myself and had for so long. The therapy helped the much needed process of integration, to discover and accept my shadow, those parts of the self that I would have preferred to disown. I think that I am more tolerant of people's anger and destructive tendencies, having learned to see and to accept my own. Therapy also helped me to recognise the power of the unconscious and how much of our behaviour is motivated without awareness. I think that all these aspects of my own therapy help me to be more connected to clients.

These were positive aspects of the work, but there were other aspects that were less so. I hated the way in which simple questions were turned into material for analysis. I did not like the absence of any kind of working agreement or information, that I could use to make sensible choices. The process emphasised my pathology and was very frightening because of that. I also thought that there should have been some initial discussion about what might be entailed in this form of work.

Based on this experience, I am sensitive to power issues in any form of professional practice. I give myself quite a hard time, in fact, as I struggle with this theme. For example, I am aware of the costs to a client of being in any form of psychological treatment, costs in terms of time and inconvenience and the anxiety of sometimes having a taken-for-granted world and set of assumptions turned upside down. In my practice I am as open as I possibly can be. If a patient asks a question, I will do my best to answer it truthfully.

I have written rather more under this heading of trauma than other sections, and I suppose that is because the experience of Catherine's illness was so influential in the way my life developed following her death. Quite apart from changing the direction of my career, Catherine's short life has facilitated my capacity to empathise, and to enter into communion with people who are in the deepest levels of unspeakable despair. I cannot *know* what they are going through; no other human being can; their experiences are unique. But I do have the facility to listen, to accept and to withstand the expression of their pain without being overwhelmed by it. I have compassion, and for that I am thankful.

Afterword

I did go on to have another daughter, born four months after Catherine died. She, in her turn, in the year 2000, gave birth to a son. Both daughter and grandchild are well, and hold a very special place in my heart.

References

Eliot, T.S. (1935) *The Cocktail Party*. In *The Complete Poems and Plays of T.S. Eliot*. London: Faber.

Erskine, R. (1997) *Methods of an Integrative Psychotherapy*. San Francisco: TA Publications.

Miller, A. (1949) *Death of a Salesman*. London: Penguin.

Shaw, C. (1930) *The Jack Roller: A Delinquent Boy's Own Story*. Chicago: University of Chicago Press.

10

The Nursing Perspective

'Pain is the Breaking of the Shell that Encases your Understanding'

Kahlil Gibran 1926

Kevin Yates

My legs swung between the legs of the 1970s tubular chrome dining room chair. I was sitting next to my seven-year-old brother, eighteen months my senior, with an array of toy soldiers scattered around the table. My mother, the font of all knowledge, was serving up our dinner. 'Something very sad happened last night,' she announced as she spooned the baked beans onto the plate. Silence fell over the table as we pondered the word 'sad'. Had we run out of chocolate biscuits again, or had my action man with eagle eyes got caught in the vacuum cleaner again and not made it in one piece through his ordeal? 'Last night,' continued my mother as she further extended her maternal duties to the equal distribution of chips, 'Great Granmare died and went to heaven.' Sad, died, and went to heaven – such a complicated mixture of words. I wanted to be sure my brother, Christopher, didn't get more chips than I did but now I had two things to concentrate on. 'Did a cowboy shoot her?' asked Christopher. 'No darling a cowboy didn't shoot her, she just went to sleep and whilst she was sleeping the baby Jesus came to take her to heaven and she died.'

It was all very complicated but I was actually quite an expert at this 'died and went to heaven' thing. After all, Fred, my beloved hamster, had experienced the very same thing. As he had escaped my loving clutches and scuttled under the boiler, he had come across a particularly irresistible red electric cable and sunk his shiny teeth into the centre of this juicy morsel. As the sparks leapt from the little furry Fred, my mother had explained that Fred was dead and incidentally, I heard her tell my father, we might need a new boiler! My eyes filled with tears as I realised that I would never again be able to share my cornflakes with Fred. Breakfast time would never be the same again. The more I contemplated life without Fred the more inconsolable I became.

Fortunately for all concerned (apart from Fred) it was a Saturday morning and after a relatively short grieving process my father arrived home with a little cardboard box housing a brand new, fitter, slimmer and altogether more friendly Fred look-alike. Fred Mk II had arrived, and as he made himself at home in the little Fred house, all in the world was well. As I tucked into my chips I had an uneasy feeling that this was different and although I couldn't be completely certain, I wasn't expecting Dad to come home with a cardboard box housing a new fitter, slimmer Great Granmare, so I didn't cry, but I did finish off all my chips.

Eighteen months later something very sad did happen. My friend's dad died and by now I knew that this was a terrible thing to happen. Andrew, my friend cried every day at school and it seemed to me that this was an altogether different experience than that which I had encountered in my seven years. The school would gather every morning and pray for Andrew's father. It was announced after one assembly that some of the school would be attending the funeral but only those from junior four, the eldest year. I felt thoroughly cheated by this exclusion, as we had recently learnt a great deal about dying. Easter was not long past. I had heard all about Jesus dying on the cross to enable the rest of us to live. The continuing story that I was particularly interested in was the fascinating part where Jesus ascended into heaven. Our teacher had been very clear about this enthralling story line. Jesus had died and then risen from the dead. Only Jesus could rise from the dead of course, that went without saying, but then after meeting up with all his friends again he looked up to heaven and floated upwards into the clouds ultimately ending up in Heaven, a really nice place by all accounts. I was so envious that year four would get to see this and I was to be left wondering what it would be like to see the coffin lid open and Andrew's dad float up out of the coffin and make his way through the church roof ultimately winging his way to heaven. Life is just so unfair.

I journeyed through the following years unscathed by sadness and grief. My closest friend in the world was Stephen, my other brother, 17 years my senior. During these formative years, Stephen was my father figure, big brother and dearest friend. I spent all my spare time with Stephen. I idolised him. My aim in life was simply to grow up to be like him in every way. I couldn't have been happier than when I was with Stephen until one day, when I was 14 years old, he collapsed and had a fit. My life was about to change so dramatically in a way I could never have comprehended.

The Catholic influence on my life was always present and I considered this to be positive. The nuns who taught me guided me through my education in a loving style and supported me as I grew up with the knowledge of Stephens's illness. I had been told that Stephen had a 'scar' on his brain, probably caused by a sports injury; I had no reason to doubt this diagnosis. Having been brought up to believe that if we wanted something, all we had to do was ask God, I had endeavoured to stay in touch with God to and make sure that he was fully aware of my wants. For a couple of years I journeyed through life unaware how gravely ill Stephen was, but as disease progressed within his brain it became increasingly clear that things were not going to return to normal. I discovered the truth; a tumour was slowly growing inside Stephens's brain that couldn't be reached by a surgeon's knife or any of my prayers. My faith was to be tested beyond my comprehension. The presence of illness continued to dominate my life. Undoubtedly, this presence nurtured my inherent ability to care, an instinct and a desire that precipitated my decision, at the age of 18, to embark upon nurse training.

Historically, academic studies were not my forte. However, I displayed an identifiable and impressive skill when dealing with distressed patients and their families. I was unleashed and dizzy with my first experience of success and achievement. It remains curious, however, that I never attended lectures that might inadvertently touch upon the topic of brain tumours. Although not a conscious decision, I distanced myself from the entire scope of brain tumour symptoms, pathology, treatment and prognosis. My avoidance strategy served me well until just six weeks prior to my twenty-first birthday when I received an unexpected telephone call from my mother. Stephen was dead.

As I sat in the cold draughty lobby of the nurses' home, pain like I had never felt before enveloped my entire body. The telephone receiver hung from the pay phone. I crouched to the floor, held my head in my hands and howled, uncontrollably and unashamedly, without consideration of any noise that I made. I screamed as my body fought with the pain and tried to reject it. So desperately I tried to dismiss the torture that was taking over me. I failed. The strength of the beast was overwhelming and without question. I was helpless and totally at the mercy of grief, the most unkind and unwelcome of visitors so far to enter into my life. Grief now occupied a space in my life, a space previously occupied so lovingly by Stephen. What would I do without him? I became locked in a world where my only weapon against the pain and hurt I experienced was total disbelief and numbness.

As I followed the hearse in the dark of a January evening I truly could not believe that Stephen could possibly be inside the coffin. This disbelief was to come to an end as we arrived at the church and I took my place behind the hearse to carry the coffin. As I raised the oak casket to my shoulders shock swept over me, the weight, it was so heavy, the hard edging so beautifully carved cutting into my shoulder and neck. I struggled along with the five other bearers to negotiate the steps up to the church entrance and finally I had to acknowledge that Stephen really was inside the coffin. My final memory of that day is carrying Stephen from the church to his grave. The final act of love I could offer was to lower him into the ground and the only words I remember being spoken were those from the Song of Songs: 'So come, come with me my love, my dove, for winter has ended and springtime is here, 'tis time indeed for sweet, sweet singing'.

Little did I know that Stephen would be the very special person who, in dominating my life by his absence, not only would influence my ability to care for others, but would also determine my future life in palliative care and offer me the chance to enter into the lives of many others.

For the following three years I worked with drive and dedication, though the concept of reflective practice was alien to me. I did not stop to think about what was driving me and how ambition was affecting my personal life. Surgical oncology was followed by medical oncology and haematology. I was drawn deeper and deeper into the world of oncology and yet without exception my time was spent developing a palliative care approach towards the most needy of patients. As I still had not discovered reflective practice, unbeknown to me I was entering 'tiger territory' as far as my career and personal life were concerned. The pain I was living with following Stephens's death was as great as it had ever been and I was not consciously aware just how much this was influencing my life. That was about to change.

I was on night duty the week that the third anniversary of Stephens's death fell. I had made it to the end of my seventh night and as usual there were too many patients and not enough nurses. I was the only qualified nurse on duty in a 38-bedded oncology unit within a large London teaching hospital and at 6am I was well into my final drug round of the week. The patients were so very poorly and many of them deeply afraid. Bells were ringing throughout the unit and I was inundated with requests to give morphine and to give it quickly. As the patients were wakening they were wakening with pain and I knew it was going to take over an hour to get around the 38 patients. I was less than half way around the ward when I entered the side room of a young patient, a 42-year-old woman, a primary school teacher, widowed with two small children. I entered the room offering my usual good morning and made my way to the end of the bed for the drug chart. 'I've been thinking a lot about dying,' the woman told me. I froze for a split second and looked into her tear filled eyes. 'I'm so scared,' she said. I could see the fear in her eyes that she was admitting to. So many things shot through my mind in what must have only been a fraction of a second; no other staff nurse on the ward, 20 more patients needing analgesia, the breakfasts hadn't been given out, and the day staff would be here in less than 30 minutes. 'Have you?' I said. 'I'll get your tablets for you.' I dispensed the medication, went back into the side room and shot off with my drug trolley. I didn't go back to the patient. Ten years later, I feel such guilt as I put these words to paper. To the lady whom I failed on that January morning, I am so very sorry. It was not that I could not deal with the situation nor that I could not find the right words to comfort her. I simply did not have time to care. And yet I did care. I cared very deeply and I cried as I travelled home on the train. I never returned to that ward again.

The following day I was still very upset at my failing to care enough. I felt exhausted both physically and mentally. Tears flowed freely on and off during the day but as I had several days away from work, I was sure I would gather myself together. As the days passed I did not improve, in fact, things got worse. As my distress gathered pace it became clear to me that my real distress was not about the woman in the side room. I was focusing on my own loss of three years. It was not only the patient in the side room that I had failed, it was Stephen. As I entered a phase of reflection, I could see that I was living out both my grief and also the denial of my pain through my work. This took some time and soul-searching to discover, and I engaged the professional help of a psychotherapist to enable me to fully unravel and understand myself. As I worked with my mind I greeted a new visitor into my life, not a visitor I welcomed nor one to whom I knew how to respond. Depression had infiltrated my world and for the first time it seemed that the visitor was taking over.

> I stood in a clinical corridor, lino flooring and tiled walls. The smell of hospital all around me. A small window looked into a vaguely lit room that housed a bed. I entered the room alone and silence filled the air. The room was still and the presence of death hung heavily. As I ventured deeper into the room, I could sense Stephen. He was covered on the bed and though I knew why I was there I could not actually believe my presence was necessary. Moving forward, my heart pounding, I trembled with fear and battled with the churning sensation that was rising from deep within me. Stephen lay motionless on the bed, his face exposed, his red hair freshly combed. The dim lighting barely allowed me to see his heavily freckled skin. I stood over the bed listening to the inner scream from my soul calling out in desperation. I don't want to be here; I don't want to see this; I don't want this to be happening. As if in a scene from a film, I was looking down at myself within the room, watching my own sadness, wanting to comfort myself, yet unable to reach out. Back inside my own body, I reached out and touched Stephen's face. I jumped with such shock as the cold sensation crept through my fingertips and the knowledge of his death was confirmed within my brain. As I wept inconsolably I reached out again and held Stephen's face. How could he be dead? His body looked so young, so healthy and yet he was icy cold. I moved back the sheet to reveal his hand. As I placed mine next to his, I closed my

eyes. He grabbed me suddenly and I opened my eyes to see Stephen's face, discoloured, his decomposing flesh was twisted in torturous pain and his hand was gripping mine so tightly I could not break free. I screamed with sheer panic and the scream woke me, crying, sweating, and alone at home some three years after Stephen had died. This dream called on me night after night so frequently that I became fearful of sleep and would do all I could to avoid going to my bed.

My need for help was clear, yet depression was shrouding my ability to acknowledge that need. I visited my doctor to discuss a sick note, having no intention of explaining what was happening. Fortunately for me, a few gentle questions and my plight tumbled out. I needed some time away from the world of death and dying. Yet this wasn't to be 'time off'. I had a lot of work to do for 'Me'.

During the following three months I visited my therapist weekly, travelling back in my mind into my childhood and exploring what my bereavement was truly about. Working alongside a professional guide I was able to face that which I had never before accepted. Stephen was gone and would never return. Though I had consciously known this since I felt the weight of the coffin embedded in my shoulder, I came to realise that, subconsciously, I was waiting to see him, talk with him and explain all the feelings that I had been living through. In addition to playing the waiting game, I was reacting quite differently on another level. The energy and drive that I had been spending in caring for my patients was about more than my being a nurse. It was about my desire to relive all the aspects of Stephen's death that I had not been included in. In ensuring that information was given to patients and their families at appropriate times and with appropriate detail, I was trying to recreate the information that I was denied. I wanted to be sure that others were prepared as I had never been prepared. I wanted to ensure that others had the opportunity to say their goodbyes unlike myself. I wanted others to be present at their loved ones' death as I had not been. My life's work so far was to ensure that others did not end up trapped in their nightmare as I was.

As I accepted the reality of where I was emotionally, I began to experience the freedom of my own life. Accepting and understanding why I operated as I did presented me with many options previously unacknowledged. I ceased to relive day after day my own lack of information around Stephens's illness, my own desire to say goodbye to someone I loved so very deeply and to be present at his death in order to care for him. I wrote a letter to Stephen saying all that I wished I had been able to say before he died, how much I loved him, how much I admired him. I also wrote in great detail the recurring nightmare of my visiting his body. I left the letter and the details of the nightmare under his photograph overnight and the following day I burnt them. I have never had the nightmare again. In fact, within a couple of weeks I dreamt about being with Stephen. It was a pleasant dream of happy times and though I wakened crying as I realised it was only a dream, I was able to shed tears whilst remembering a joyful event in my life. My sadness diminished as did my depression; I was in control again and my visitor was invited to leave.

Once again I was ready to return to my passion, caring for the dying patient. I was, however, not going back. I was most definitely moving forward with a new and deeper understanding of who I was and of the particular gifts that I had. These gifts were to be used to their full potential within my career. I had discovered reflective practice and was now able to grow and develop to a greater depth. Taking employment within a busy and well-respected oncology unit, I gained my post-registration certificate in oncology nursing. During this year I continued to develop my reflective skills working with a clinical supervisor and ensuring that I both cared for myself and reached my full potential. Though I had great affection for the world of oncology my gifts lay within the field of palliative care and I decided to move into the hospice world. I was employed as a clinical nurse specialist in palliative care and many new challenges lay ahead.

For six years I cared for untold numbers of people who were living with life-limiting disease. I told patients they were going to die, wives what to expect in the final days of their husbands' lives and children that their mother or father had just died. I did not find the work difficult, as in each situation I was able to reflect on how I would want to be spoken to if this were happening to me, how I would want to be nursed if I were lying in that bed, how I would want someone to break bad news to me if they had to. Moving from one sad house to another, possibly visiting five families a day, had its own challenges and again reflective practice and clinical supervision strengthened me. I had to learn whom the sadness belonged to. Whenever I was leaving the house of a family I was caring for, I did not take with me that which was not mine to take. The family jewels or the cash from the sideboard stayed with the family. In exactly the same way I did not take the sadness with me.

Taking this further I understood that to take on the patient's pain or that of the family was to deny them their sadness. This was their moment, and a moment that had to be lived and experienced by them. Nurses will often adopt the burden of the patient's pain with the misguided belief that it will make the patient feel better. Of course this is not the case and any transference of pain can only lead to the proliferation of the pain in question. As a professional it was my responsibility to ensure the best quality of life for the longest period of time, combining this with the best possible memories for those who were in that particular patient's life. It was vital that I allowed the sadness of others to be present in my work. Never to acknowledge such sorrow would be wrong. Our nurse training etches within our minds the need to make things better, to put right that which is causing distress, yet when faced with a 39-year-old father of two, married to someone who expected to spend the next 50 years together, how can any professional put things right?

The nurse who possesses the skills necessary to care for the dying will not hesitate to sit with the patient and say, 'Things are really awful for you at the moment', so allowing the patient to talk of their pain. 'What is the worst thing for you at the moment?' This question allows the patient to explore the immediate pain or distress they are experiencing. It is however a question that one must have the confidence to both ask and to act upon. I have often asked this question expecting the answer to be 'the pain' or 'the sickness', so allowing me to fly into action and right the problem. If we are truly offering holistic, patient-centred care, then we are asking 'What is the worst thing for you at the moment – holistically?' When the answer comes back and is, 'The television doesn't work and I have to sit all day alone with no TV,' then the true skills of the clinical nurse specialist in palliative care are unleashed. If you can arrange for a patient's TV to be repaired, ensure they have sufficient bedding in the house, arrange for meals to be delivered daily, let the dog out into the garden, assess the patient's physical, emotional and spiritual pain, advise on necessary medication changes, contact the general practitioner and suggest several different medications for the patient, discuss with the patient the fact that time is getting short and life may be coming to an end, remember to let the dog back into the house, ensure that you leave the sadness behind you and then move on to the next patient and start again in the knowledge that there will be at least another four patients that will need your help today in coping with their sadness – then you would make a good community palliative care nurse.

The idea that there is 'nothing more we can do for you' has always both horrified and angered me. I have met so many patients who were 'dismissed' from hospital as if they were failures, with this very message. This is never the case and, when faced with this scenario, my reply will always be the same: 'There is something we can do for you and there always will be, we can always care for you.'

Caring for the dying patient is not just about controlling their pain and obliterating their nausea. As individuals we are more than mechanical beings that hurt and vomit. As unique beings, we possess the deepest and most complex of emotions and one emotion offered very little nurturing is that of hope. I have discussed with many health care professionals the issue of hope and the importance of hope in the lives of those we care for. Often this is 'dodged' as a tricky and fearful subject and the opinion of many would be that it is wrong to offer hope to those who are actually doomed. Hope is one of the most important issues in quality of life as without hope, what are we?

The real difficulty is that to truly offer hope to our patients, we as professionals have to first offer honesty. Honesty will always expose our vulnerability and that makes life unpredictable and rather scary. In palliative care there is a re-focusing of the emphasis of hope. Hope and honesty become a collaboration, which in turn can aid the stability and presence of quality. Hope last year may have been that the patient recovered from bowel cancer and returned to a healthy and fulfilled life style. Today things may have changed and hope may be that he feels well and has sufficient energy to enjoy a final Christmas with the children. Further along the journey hope may again have altered in its offerings. Today hope may be that the patient can eat a little and not feel sick or that the pain does not wake him in the night. Wherever hope lies, nobody has the right to deny it of a patient. As each target of hope is reached, a sense of achievement and satisfaction belongs to the patient; this satisfaction in turn affords fulfilment. Hope is as much the property of the patient as are the family jewels, the money on the sideboard and the sadness in the house.

As my passion for ensuring that quality care is offered to those most in need developed further, I came to realise that there needed to be a change in my life if I were to reach out to those within the sphere of my influence. As a community palliative care nurse I could ensure that those in my care received such quality but there were many more and the only way to access this group was by accessing those who delivered the care. I moved into the field of management within palliative care. Though leaving 'hands on' patient care behind me, I was driven by the fact that I could now influence the care others offered. Moving away from the work of the clinical nurse specialist was a painful experience and one that I also grieved for. I did however feel a strong sense of confirmation that this was the way forward. Now, some years later, I am director of nursing at Saint Joseph's Hospice in Hackney. It is one of the oldest and certainly the largest hospice in the country and though I no longer sit with patients and guide them through the final weeks of their lives, I am in a position to ensure that the same care I would always have given can be afforded to those patients whom we as an organisation care for.

My journey through bereavement and pain has ultimately brought me great gifts. Stephen died and disaster struck my life with nothing but the certainty that no good could ever come from such a tragedy. My certainty was misplaced. The suffering and pain that was a part of my previous life has been the carving of the depth of my life today. It may be confusing for some to talk of the wounded healer as my aim ultimately is not to offer healing *per se*. It is, however, to offer healing for the moment and that demands understanding and acceptance of whatever the place is in your life where you find yourself today.

Reference

Gibran, K. (1926) *The Prophet*. New York: Wordsworth.

11

Overview

Christina Mason

These are the stories of nine men and women who have spent many years working with people who are in distress. The questions I asked of them were the same; what led you into the work and what has been the effect of this unique journey on the way you practice? Except in the case of myself, of course, I had no idea what would emerge in answer to these questions. I was fascinated to read each account as it was sent on to me. Most of the authors remarked how helpful the process of reviewing their professional lives had been. The words of Julia sum up the tone of several who remarked on the exercise: 'It has given me the opportunity to remember the joys, the disappointments, the highs and the lows, the regrets and the achievements.'

There are substantial differences in these stories, as is to be expected. I would like to think that the nine accounts speak for themselves and that the different aspects of the writers' stories will stimulate each reader according to his or her own biography. There are, however, some common themes arising and I will identify these in the paragraphs that follow.

The 'outsider'

Five of the writers describe the experience of being or feeling like an outsider, although the reasons for this sense are of course different. As I was reading the accounts, I wondered if occupying an 'outsider' position drew people in a particular way to work with those who are dying and who are suffering the pain of loss. The idea of 'outsider' resonates with several illness themes. For example, the subject of death and dying used to be described as the 'last taboo' (Gorer 1965) and several authors have discussed the stigma associated with illness (Goffman 1963; Field 1976; Sontag 1978). C. S. Lewis, writing about his experience following the death of his wife, reports feeling an embarrassment to everyone he met. (Lewis 1961). In my own experience I remember going to work at a residential home for people with cerebral palsy. It was well equipped and its site was idyllic in some respects, but it was 'outside' the walls of the city and on the banks of a river that regularly overflowed its banks. In the same way the old style large mental hospitals were often built in gracious parklands, but well out of sight of those who were deemed to be sane. Is there any doubt what the 'collective unconscious' was saying here?

Connected with the idea of the 'outsider' is the notion of being 'different'. People who are extremely ill or who have disabilities are often seen to be 'different' and have frequently been the subject of discrimination in employment, housing, and so on. Four of the writers of these chapters highlight their awareness of difference, experiencing the pain of exclusion because of skin colour in the case of one, and the others strongly empathising, for reasons connected with their histories, with the plight of those seen to be unjustly treated.

The wounded healer

Eight of the people whose stories are told here experienced difficult situations of loss, illness or trauma prior to taking up their chosen careers. They may be examples of the 'wounded healers' that I referred to in chapter one. Even though the precise details of the difficulties they experienced are different, all appear to have played an important part in the motivation to care for others. As a doctor, Louis treats people who suffer symptoms he himself has suffered. David is very clear in his story of the influence of childhood losses on his work in palliative care. Gordon 'found' himself conducting research which has drawn attention to the pain of loss, his family having experienced the loss of a daughter before he was born. Similarly, Julia went back into new work with people who were very ill, following the death of her mother and the redundancy of her husband. Even where the career choice was not deliberately made as a result of early experience, it seems to me that there may have been unconscious motivation playing its part. As Sir Peter Medawar (1967) wrote, 'chance favours the prepared mind'. People can look for remedies for their pain but, as in the case of the legendary Chiron, others are healed in the process of their search. In the case of seven of the writers here, such had been their experience of care that they have made purposeful attempts to improve the service given to others.

The use of the self

Five of the writers described long journeys in therapy, to find their true selves in some cases, and in others to look at unresolved past issues. These journeys have sometimes been painful but they have been formative in the way the writers work as professionals. One found a way of using his experience of depressions to enhance his understanding of the despair frequently entered into by people as they consider the ends of their lives. A second, having come to terms with her own destructive impulses, is now more able to 'stay alongside' and, without fear, work with those people who are terribly angry about their mortal illness. Another has come to understand some of his less 'desirable' personality attributes and to convert them into therapeutic strengths. The fourth writer needed to go deep into her past, nearly going mad in the process, but finding the therapeutic method so helpful to her own healing that she dedicated herself and her career to helping others on their own journeys of discovery. The fifth experienced incapacitating depression but through the therapy that followed learned how the unresolved feelings following the loss of someone much loved was distorting his practice.

In some ways, it is not surprising that there are links between these therapeutic journeys and the way in which the writers have brought themselves into the work they do. What I found more unexpected were the other influences identified. Who could have predicted that the work of illustration could impact on work with the dying, but Lois certainly made use of the earlier patience she required in this work during her later vocation. Robin's life in the village shop taught him about service as well as sowing the seeds for learning about communication. My experience of performing music provided me with a model of communication. Louis and Lois describe their appreciation of mystery and the spiritual dimension, which has helped them as they approach patients' uncertainties at the ends of their lives. Julia found a constructive way, through client advocacy, of channelling her anger.

It seems to me in reading the stories of these nine authors, that almost every aspect of life experience *can* be used in professional life, and used in a creative, helpful way. However, some of these life experiences and personal attributes may not be discovered without the opportunity to introspect and to consider the question 'who am I and what do I bring to my work?' I believe that it is important to reflect on how our personal styles have come into being, and to explore ways in which previously unused aspects of our total selves can be developed.

I have tried in my own work to follow the example of Carl Rogers (1961), who suggested that the greatest gift we have to offer in the work of healing is wholeness. The words of Remen (1996) on this theme are poignant, and I hope that readers of this book will take time to consider the ways in which their own selves and life experiences can be used in new ways:

> The healing of our present woundedness may lie in recognising and reclaiming the capacity we all have to heal each other, the enormous power in the simplest human relationships: the strength of a touch, the blessing of forgiveness, the grace of someone taking you just as you are and finding in you an unexpected goodness. (p.217)

Working with the dying

I don't think I am any more able than others to provide clear answers to the questions so often asked by neighbours, family and friends of those working with people who are dying and grieving. How do you manage with all the distress that you witness? This group of nine professionals has learned how important it is to recognise the impact of the work on their own everyday functioning. The work *is* difficult and all the writers of these chapters have needed to find methods of dealing with the stresses involved. Walking, music, art, poetry, formal supervision, humour, talking; all of these activities have been found to be helpful. Perhaps more importantly, the writers have learned to recognise and accept that they do have strong feelings about the people with whom they work, and that if time is not taken to look at these emotional responses, there are likely to be problems at some later date.

Although we may hope that it might, the very frequency of contact with distress does not insulate or give protection when members of our own families are ill or we contemplate our own mortality. It is probably the case that the transition from life to death remains an extraordinary event and certainly for me, there remain many unanswered questions and mysteries which lie at the heart of life as well as death.

I sense that there will always be a tension in reflecting on these central issues, whether we are sitting in the armchair and contemplating the 'meaning of it all' at the end of an evening, or working in the 'thick of it' during the day. What I mean by this is that I see an irreconcilable tension between explanation and understanding in any discipline and the experience of the phenomena about which theories are elaborated. Problems arise when the findings of various disciplines are seen not for what they are – analyses of phenomena at a particular level – but the whole truth. It is the sort of tension that is spoken of by Louis, one of the contributors to this book, when he describes the scene in the dissecting room, the 'cool beauty of science' contrasted with the raw, direct experience of life. Likewise, the description of the first movement of Bach's Passion according to St Matthew as simultaneously ritornello, fugue and chorale prelude is an analysis at a particular level; it will never encompass, nor does it intend to encompass, the experiential grasp of the piece as a miracle. The isolation of the enzyme deficiency responsible for Tay-Sach's disease is a biological finding; it says nothing, since it intends to say nothing about the suffering attendant on that disease. The working assumption of physiologists studying the brains of animals is that consciousness has a corresponding neural activity; it is the mechanism of thinking and not the experience of it that can be explained in the activity of many millions of cells.

All of us I think need to stay alive to this tension in our work, whether it is based in a palliative care setting or in any other kind of environment dedicated to the relief of human suffering. And here it is that I end with the wish that the stories, experiences and ideas contained in this book will lead to ongoing reflection on the personal and the professional and their interrelationships.

References

Field, D. (1976) 'The social definition of illness.' In D. Tuckett (ed) *An Introduction to Medical Sociology*. London: Tavistock.

Goffman, E. (1963) *Stigma: Notes on the Management of a Spoiled Identity*. New Jersey: Prentice Hall.

Gorer, G. (1965) *Death, Grief and Mourning in Contemporary Britain*. London: Cresset.

Lewis, C.S. (1961) *A Grief Observed*. London: Faber.

Medawar, P. (1967) *The Art of the Soluble: Creativity and Originality in Science*. London: Methuen.

Remen, R. (1996) *Kitchen Table Wisdom*. New York: Riverhead Books.

Rogers, C. (1961) *On Becoming a Person: A Therapist's View of Psychotherapy*. London: Constable.

Sontag, S. (1978) *Illness as Metaphor*. London: Penguin Books.

Follow-up questions

You may find the following questions useful to consider on your own or in a group:

1. What age were you when you first thought you would like to do the work you do today?

2. Was there anything that led you to be interested in this sort of work? What was this?

3. What expectations did you have of this work as a career?

4. During your training for this career did you receive any advice about the management of feelings in doing this kind of work? Did you find this advice helpful?

5. What are the most difficult aspects of your work?

6. Who or what gives you support in your work? Do you receive regular clinical or professional supervision?

7. Do you think that the reasons that brought you into this work influence the way you practise? In what way?

Details of Contributors

Gillie Bolton works in Sheffield University, based in the Department of General Practice as a senior research fellow in Medical Humanities. Her speciality is the use of creative writing in therapeutic work and in professional practice and development. Gillie has written extensively about her work and spoken to many audiences. In addition she is an established poet.

Julia Franklin is a pioneer in the area of palliative care social work, being a powerful influence on the development of this specialist discipline, especially in the formation of the Association of Hospice and Palliative Care Social Workers. Julia has retired from full-time practice now but for several years she has been a consultant and supervisor to several hospices and palliative care teams.

Louis Heyse-Moore is the medical director of St Joseph's Hospice, Hackney, London. He has also worked at St Christopher's Hospice and Trinity Hospice, and before becoming a specialist in palliative care was a general practitioner. He has published the results of his research in a number of academic journals and has taken a particular interest in the spiritual aspects of palliative care and complementary therapies.

Christina Mason is a social worker and psychotherapist. She has been working at St Joseph's Hospice in Hackney, East London for the past six years, combining both of these professions in her work with patients, relatives and staff. Prior to moving to London, she worked in various hospitals and also in a general practice setting in Scotland. Before social work, Christina was a researcher and academic lecturer for 19 years in the medical schools of Nottingham and Dundee University. In this capacity she has published on the effect of illness on patients and their carers.

David Oliviere is the director of education at St Christopher's Hospice, Sydenham, London. Prior to this he was a lecturer in palliative care social work at Middlesex University, building on his skills and experience of practice in several hospice environments. David has lectured extensively internationally and has taken a particular interest in ethnicity and palliative care. He has many publications to his name including a book co-authored with Rosalind Hargreaves and Barbara Monroe reflecting his knowledge and experience in psychosocial palliative care.

Lois Pollock was born in Australia and moved to Britain where she qualified as a social worker in her early adult life. She has extensive knowledge and understanding of the needs of people with life-limiting illness, based on work in several communities and countries. Lois has a particular vocation to respond to the spiritual needs of people, and this is also expressed in her work as an integrative psychotherapist. Lois has recently returned to Australia and is managing professionals working with older persons, many of whom are survivors of the Holocaust.

Gordon Riches works as a researcher and university teacher in sociology at the University of Derby and has used a sociological perspective to reflect on findings from his research with people who grieve the loss of a child. Gordon has an extensive publication list which has included his book co-authored with Pam Dawson, *An Intimate Loneliness*.

Robin Trewartha is a freelance chartered counselling psychologist. He has knowledge and experience of trauma and loss, having had many years of work with adults and children in the probation and child protection services in several parts of the country. Robin has also worked as a university teacher and has a great deal of experience as an educator. He has published papers in a number of different fields of professional practice, including a book on managing violence and aggression co-authored with David Leadbetter.

Kevin Yates was appointed director of nursing at St Joseph's Hospice, Hackney, London, in 2001. He has brought to this post a long-term commitment to the needs of those who are sick and dying. He has experience in oncology nursing and of palliative care nursing both in hospice and the community and sees reflective practice as being central to this work.

Subject Index

Author Index